DUE

MIDDLE EAST NATIONS IN THE NEWS

Iran
IN THE NEWS

PAST, PRESENT, AND FUTURE

Amy Graham

MyReportLinks.com Books
an imprint of

 Enslow Publishers, Inc.
Box 398, 40 Industrial Road
Berkeley Heights, NJ 07922
USA

MyReportLinks.com Books, an imprint of Enslow Publishers, Inc. MyReportLinks®
is a registered trademark of Enslow Publishers, Inc.

Library of Congress Cataloging-in-Publication Data

Graham, Amy.
  Iran in the news : past, present, and future / Amy Graham.
     p. cm. — (Middle East nations in the news)
  Includes bibliographical references and index.
  ISBN 1-59845-022-0
  1. Iran—Juvenile literature. I. Title. II. Series.
  DS254.5.G65 2006
  955—dc22

                                    2005018777

Printed in the United States of America

10 9 8 7 6 5 4 3 2 1

To Our Readers:
Through the purchase of this book, you and your library gain access to the Report Links that specifically back
up this book.
The Publisher will provide access to the Report Links that back up this book and will keep these Report Links
up to date on **www.myreportlinks.com** for five years from the book's first publication date.
We have done our best to make sure all Internet addresses in this book were active and appropriate when we
went to press. However, the author and the Publisher have no control over, and assume no liability for, the
material available on those Internet sites or on other Web sites they may link to.
The usage of the MyReportLinks.com Books Web site is subject to the terms and conditions stated on the Usage
Policy Statement on **www.myreportlinks.com.**
A password may be required to access the Report Links that back up this book. The password is found on the
bottom of page 4 of this book.
Any comments or suggestions can be sent by e-mail to comments@myreportlinks.com or to the address on the
back cover.

Contents

Persian carpets

Shrine of Hazrat Fatimeh

MyReportLinks.com Books
Great Books, Great Links, Great for Research!

The Internet sites featured in this book can save you hours of research time. These Internet sites—we call them **"Report Links"**—are constantly changing, but we keep them up to date on our Web site.

When you see this "Approved Web Site" logo, you will know that we are directing you to a great Internet site that will help you with your research.

Give it a try! Type **http://www.myreportlinks.com** into your browser, click on the series title and enter the password, then click on the book title, and scroll down to the Report Links listed for this book.

The Report Links will bring you to great source documents, photographs, and illustrations. MyReportLinks.com Books save you time, feature Report Links that are kept up to date, and make report writing easier than ever! A complete listing of the Report Links can be found on pages 116–117 at the back of the book.

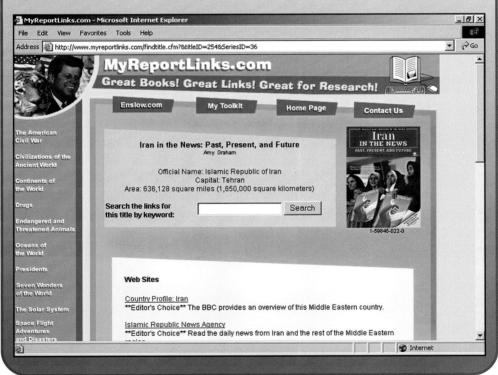

Please see "To Our Readers" on the copyright page for important information about this book, the MyReportLinks.com Web site, and the Report Links that back up this book.

Please enter **NIN1262** if asked for a password.

▲ Map of Iran

▷ **Flag**
Iran's tri-colored flag has green, white, and red stripes. The tulip, Iran's national emblem, stands in the white center. Allah Akbar, or "God is Great," is written in white Arabic letters, eleven times on the bottom of the green stripe and eleven times at the top of the red stripe.

▷ **Official Name**
Islamic Republic of Iran

▷ **Capital**
Tehran

▷ **Population**
68,017,860 (July 2005 estimate)

▷ **Area**
636,128 square miles

▷ **Highest Point**
Mount Damavand at 18,606 feet above sea level

▷ **Lowest Point**
Caspian Sea at 92 feet below sea level

▷ **Location**
On the Persian Gulf, Gulf of Oman, and the Caspian Sea, between Iraq and Pakistan

▷ **Head of State**
Supreme Leader Seyed Ayatollah Ali Khamenei

▷ **Head of Government**
President Mahmud Ahmadi-Nejad

▷ **Monetary Unit**
The Iranian rial. 8,994 RIALS = 1 $US (July 2005)

▷ **Official Language**
Farsi (in English referred to as Persian)

▷ **National Anthem**
Islamic Republic of Iran National Anthem

▷ **National Emblem**
The word Allah (God) forms the shape of a tulip, a symbol of both martyrdom and renewal. Martyrs give up their lives to further the cause of Islam.

▷ **Religion(s)**
Shi'a Muslim (89 percent), Sunni Muslim (9 percent), Zoroastrian, Jewish, Christian, and Baha'i (2 percent)

▷ **Life Expectancy**
68 years for men, 71 years for women

▷ **National Holidays**
February 11, Revolution Day

March 21, Norouz (New Year's)

April 1, Republic Day

August 5, Constitutional Monarchy Day

Time Line

2700–644 B.C.	Kingdom of Elam is the first known civilization in Iran.
550 B.C.	Cyrus the Great founds the earliest Persian Empire.
331 B.C.	Persia falls to Macedonian king Alexander the Great.
A.D. 224	Sassanian Empire begins, reestablishing Persian control.
570–632	Life of the Prophet Muhammad.
642	Muslim Arabs win control of Persia.
819–1005	Samanid Empire melds Persian and Muslim cultures together.
1219	Ghengis Khan leads the Mongol invasion of Persia.
1501–1732	Safavid rulers restore Persian Empire.
1797–1921	Rule of the Qajar dynasty.
1804–1828	Russia and Persia battle over land.
1906	Constitution adopted, establishing the parliament.
1914	WWI begins; Russia and Britain occupy Persia.
1925	Military leader Reza Shah takes the thrown; Pahlavi dynasty begins.
1935	Persia's name changed to Iran.
1941	WWII Allied Forces remove Reza Shah from power.
1942	The shah's son, Reza Mohammad, takes the throne.
1953	U.S. Central Intelligence Agency helps the shah remove Prime Minister Mossadegh.
1978	Street protesters killed in the Black Friday Massacre.
1979	Shah overthrown in a revolution; Ayatollah Khomeini establishes Islamic Republic of Iran.
1980–1988	Iran-Iraq War.
1981	American hostages are released after 444 days in captivity.
1989	Death of Ayatollah Khomeini.
1997	Iranians elect President Mohammad Khatami who promises reforms.
2004	Conservative religious clerics regain control of parliament.
2005	The United States and Western European nations demand Iran halt its nuclear program.

Persepolis

Shah Abbas Hotel

Chapter 1 ▶

Iran in the News

Iran is reaching a crisis point. Iranians have the right to vote, but their government does not represent them. How can that be? Iranians can vote for their president. They vote to elect members of their *Majles,* or

▲ *These mullahs are gathered at an event to honor the late Ayatollah Khomeini. When Khomeini took power in 1979, he installed a government that was run by the religious elite.*

parliament. Yet no matter how the people vote, the true rulers of Iran remain conservative religious leaders called mullahs. The word mullah refers to an educated Muslim trained in Islamic law, who usually holds an official post with the government. Here is the catch: Only candidates approved by the Guardian Council may run for office. The people of Iran do not elect the Guardian Council. The supreme leader appoints half of its twelve members and the head of judiciary nominates the other half to be approved by the Majles. The supreme leader is a religious scholar who has final authority over every aspect of Iran's government. Iranians do not elect their supreme leader. They elect members of the Council of Experts who in turn elect him as leader. Many people in Iran are unhappy that their votes count so little, and that the most powerful person in their country is not directly elected by the people.

Pahlavi Monarchy

Before 1979, Iran's government was a monarchy. The king was Shah Mohammad Reza Pahlavi. Iranians were unhappy with life under the shah. They did not think he was doing a good job. They replaced the monarchy with a new government: the Islamic Republic of Iran. The new government was founded on the religion of Islam. Whatever their intentions, the religious leaders have not lived up to their pledges to better represent the people. Iranians now call them the "Mercedes mullahs" after the expensive cars they drive.[1] Officially, these leaders often have the title of ayatollah or hojatoleslam. These are

▲ *After the death of Ayatollah Khomeini in 1989, Seyed Ayatollah Ali Khamenei became Iran's Supreme Leader.*

religious titles similar to bishop, archbishop, or cardinal in the Catholic church. Once in control, these religious leaders grew wealthy and powerful. The ayatollahs who lead Iran silence anyone who speaks out against them.

▶ **America Takes Notice**

President George W. Bush had some harsh words for Iran in 2002. He declared Iran was part of an "axis of

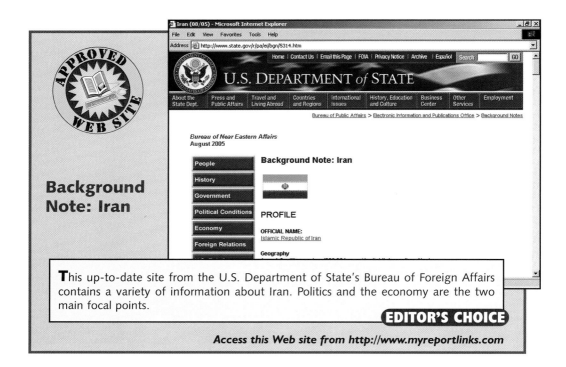

Iran (08/05) - Microsoft Internet Explorer

File   Edit   View   Favorites   Tools   Help

Address   http://www.state.gov/r/pa/ei/bgn/5314.htm

Home | Contact Us | Email this Page | FOIA | Privacy Notice | Archive | Español   Search   GO

U.S. DEPARTMENT *of* STATE

About the State Dept. | Press and Public Affairs | Travel and Living Abroad | Countries and Regions | International Issues | History, Education and Culture | Business Center | Other Services | Employment

Bureau of Public Affairs > Electronic Information and Publications Office > Background Notes

Bureau of Near Eastern Affairs
August 2005

Background Note: Iran

People

History

Government

Political Conditions

Economy

Foreign Relations

PROFILE

OFFICIAL NAME:
Islamic Republic of Iran

Geography

Background Note: Iran

This up-to-date site from the U.S. Department of State's Bureau of Foreign Affairs contains a variety of information about Iran. Politics and the economy are the two main focal points.

EDITOR'S CHOICE

Access this Web site from http://www.myreportlinks.com

evil." He accused Iran, Iraq, and North Korea of supporting terrorists.[2] Terrorists are people who scare people with violence to get what they want. Bush said these three countries were a menace to America. They mistreated their own citizens. They threatened world peace. During his first term in office (2000–04), President Bush tackled the problem of Iraq. He launched a military campaign called Operation Iraqi Freedom. American and British forces invaded Iraq. They captured its corrupt leader, Saddam Hussein. Coalition forces toppled the Iraqi government.

Yet the country of Iran, which borders Iraq on the east, was also very much on the minds of leaders in Washington, D.C. Suddenly Iran loomed as possibly the next big threat. Iran tops the United States' list of "potential trouble spots" worldwide, said Vice President Richard B. Cheney in January 2005.[3]

► Building the Bomb?

In 2002, Iran admitted it had been keeping a secret from the world. For the past eighteen years, it had worked undercover on a nuclear energy program. Iran said the goal of its nuclear program was to produce electricity. With the help of Russia, Iran was building a nuclear power plant. Once completed, the plant is designed to generate electricity. Nuclear power plants run on nuclear fuel. Iran wants to produce nuclear fuel on its own. Otherwise, it will have to depend on foreign countries for its fuel supply.

The Islamic Republic News Agency provides articles on Iran, the Middle East, and the rest of the world. Read the latest news from their Web site.

EDITOR'S CHOICE

Access this Web site from http://www.myreportlinks.com

On this Web site from *Time* magazine, you can read several articles that outline the recent history of Iran.

Access this Web site from http://www.myreportlinks.com

The United States did not believe Iran's claims. The process for making nuclear power plant fuel is the same as the one used to build a nuclear bomb. Nuclear bombs are the most destructive weapons that exist. Iran had signed a treaty agreeing it would not develop nuclear weapons. The Nuclear Non-Proliferation Treaty allows Iran to make nuclear-fueled electricity. The United States was skeptical of Iran's intentions. Why had Iran hidden its program if it was not illegal? Iran's response is that it hid the program because the sanctions made it impossible for them to legally buy needed technology. The Iranian leaders feel they need nuclear energy to better the lives of their people.

▲ Iran's leaders feel they should be able to develop nuclear power plants to provide energy for their people. The United Nations and the United States are afraid that they may use that technology to develop nuclear weapons.

▲ On January 29, 2002, in his State of the Union Address, U.S. President George W. Bush referred to the Iranian government as part of an "axis of evil" that threatens the world. This increased the tension between the United States and Iranian governments.

Since its founding in 1979, the Islamic Republic of Iran has made no secret of its hatred toward the United States. The Iranian religious leaders think the United States is an international bully. Yet the United States feels Iran is a threat. If Iran had nuclear weapons, the United States, as its number one enemy, could be in danger. Should Iran decide to strike, American soldiers in Iraq and Afghanistan would be uncomfortably close.

Other countries are concerned about Iran's secret nuclear program, too. Britain, Germany, and France are working together to solve the problem. They began diplomatic talks with Iran in 2004. Diplomacy means solving disputes by talking and compromising, not fighting wars. President Bush has said Iran must give up its nuclear program. He hopes diplomatic talks will work. The United States has not ruled out military strikes if Iran refuses. Iran has been engaged in diplomatic talks to resolve the issue, but it has said it would fight back to protect itself. In August 2004, the Iranian Defense Minister even said that if Iran thought it was about to be attacked by a foreign power, it might strike first.[4]

United Nations and the Security Council

The United Nations is made up of countries from around the world. The United Nations brings diplomats from these countries together to address world problems. The United States would like the United Nations to help shut down Iran's nuclear program. The United Nations could punish Iran by imposing sanctions. Sanctions are laws. They limit the trade a country can do with other countries. Sanctions make it difficult for people to get the products they need to live. Perhaps Iran would give up its nuclear ambitions if it faced sanctions. On the other hand, diplomacy may be working. In January 2005, Iran allowed the International Atomic Energy Agency to inspect its nuclear facilities.

Chapter 2 ▶

Introducing Iran

The Islamic Republic of Iran is located in southwest Asia. It is one of several countries that make up a region called the Middle East. Historians disagree about which countries should be considered part of the Middle East. One definition is that the Middle East stretches from Libya in northern Africa to Afghanistan in central Asia. Iran sits on the northern shore of the Persian Gulf. The Persian Gulf spills into the Arabian Sea, which opens into

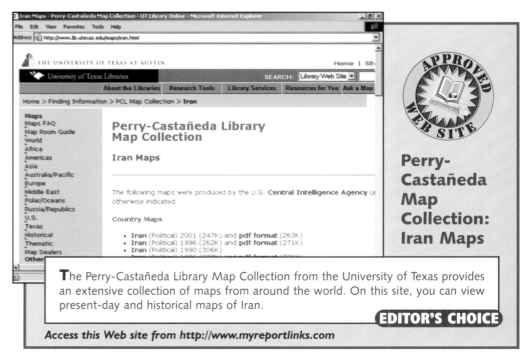

Perry-Castañeda Map Collection: Iran Maps

The Perry-Castañeda Library Map Collection from the University of Texas provides an extensive collection of maps from around the world. On this site, you can view present-day and historical maps of Iran.

EDITOR'S CHOICE

Access this Web site from http://www.myreportlinks.com

the Indian Ocean. It is an important waterway for trade to and from the Middle East. Seven countries neighbor Iran. Iraq and Turkey border it on the west. Armenia, Azerbaijan, the Caspian Sea, and Turkmenistan form the northern border. Afghanistan and Pakistan are to Iran's east. Judged by size, Iran is the sixteenth-largest nation in the world. It encompasses 636,000 square miles. The country is one-fifth the size of the United States, or slightly larger than Alaska. Imagine a map of the continental United States. Iran would fit within the area east of the Mississippi River.

A Move to the City

Iran is a breathtakingly beautiful country. It is home to rugged mountains, vast deserts, lush rain forests, and salty marshlands. Much of the terrain is rough and inhospitable. Traditionally, most of Iran's people lived in the countryside. They built oasis towns on the edge of the desert and villages on steep slopes high in the mountains. Over the last century, Iran has grown less rural. Many Iranians moved from the country into the cities. They hoped to find work and an easier way of life. Today 60 percent of Iranians live in cities. Iran's largest city is the modern capital, Tehran. Just over 12 million people, or one sixth of the total population, live in this sprawling urban center. Iran is split into thirty provinces. Although the rugged terrain and poor system of roads make travel between the regions difficult, most cities and towns are connected. People travel freely from one place to

▲ *The cities of Iran have become just as modern as the cities in the United States or other Western nations. These Iranian city dwellers are enjoying themselves at a mall.*

another. Like the individual states of the United States, each province has its own distinct culture and history.

▶ Persia: Iran's Rich Cultural Past

For thousands of years, Iran was known in the Western countries by another name: Persia. Around 550 B.C., the first Persians built a huge, wealthy empire. Over the centuries the Greeks, Romans, Arabs, Turks, Mongols, Russians, and others invaded the Persian homeland.

▲ Although there are strict limits on free speech in Iran, most people are allowed to move about freely. These people are boarding a bus for a trip to the nation of Syria.

Yet even when foreigners ruled over them, Persians kept a strong cultural identity. Persian culture is famous for beautiful poetry, luxurious rugs, and lush gardens fit for a king. In fact, the English word paradise comes from a Persian word that means enclosed garden.[1]

In 1935, Persia's king, Reza Shah Pahlavi, changed the name on all official government offices and embassies from Persia to Iran. Iran means "land of the Aryans." The Aryans were people native to Europe.

Tribes of Aryans moved into Iran, India, and southeast Asia three thousand years ago. The first Persians were one of these tribes of Aryan people. Why did Persia's king change his country's name? He wanted to modernize his country in the eyes of the world. He hoped the new name would remind the world that Persians were of European descent. His plan was to build partnerships with the emerging powers of Europe. The name Iran would set apart his country from their Arab neighbors. The name change did not really help because most people today do not connect the words Iran and Aryan. Unfortunately, people sometimes confuse Iran with Iraq, because the two names are similar. Many people did not realize that Persia and Iran were in fact the same place.[2]

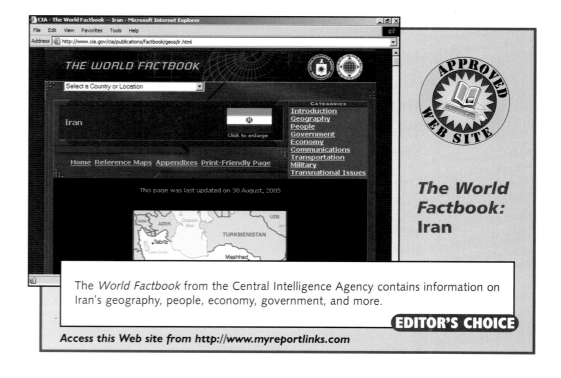

The World Factbook: Iran

The *World Factbook* from the Central Intelligence Agency contains information on Iran's geography, people, economy, government, and more.

EDITOR'S CHOICE

Access this Web site from http://www.myreportlinks.com

The People of Iran

Today nearly 70 million people live in Iran. Iranians come from different ethnic backgrounds. They speak many different languages. The official language of Iran is Farsi or Persian. The word *Farsi* refers to Persian in the Persian language. Persians make up a little over half of all Iranians. They are descendants of the ancient Aryan tribes. The next largest ethnic group is the Azeri people. Twenty-seven percent of Iranians are Azeri. The Azeri live primarily in northwestern Iran. They speak a language called Azeri Turkish. It mixes words from the Turkish and Persian languages. Ten percent of Iranians are Kurds. Like the Persians, Kurds are also descended from an ancient Aryan tribe called the Medes. Kurds and Persians follow different branches of the same religion. Kurds are Sunni Muslims, while Persians are Shi'a Muslims. Most Iranian Kurds live in the central Zagros Mountains. Kurds also live in the nearby countries of Iraq, Syria, and Turkey. Although there are large numbers of Kurds in the Middle East, they do not have their own distinct homeland. In the past, Kurds have often sought to rule themselves.

Three percent of Iranians are native Arab speakers. Most live in Khuzistan province and along the Persian Gulf. Because they tend to live in port towns, Iranian Arabs are often called bandari. *Bandar* means "port" in Persian. Two percent of Iranians belong to the Lor tribe of southwestern Iran. Lors are traditional animal herders who speak their own language called Luri. Another 2 percent are Turkmen, who live on the grasslands in northeastern Iran. Like the Kurds, Turkmen are Sunni Muslims. They wear colorful traditional dress and speak their own language. The Baluchis are Muslim desert dwellers from the provinces of Sistan and Baluchistan. Sistan and Baluchistan are on the borders of Afghanistan and Pakistan. Less than one percent of Iranians are Christians and Jews. The Assyrians are a group of Christians who live near Lake Urmia in northern Iran. Most Iranian Christians are Armenians. Armenian Christians settled in northern Iran hundreds of years ago.

The Islamic regime is not very tolerant of Judaism. The government is firmly anti-Israel. On October 26,

▲ Although their numbers are becoming fewer and fewer, there are still some nomadic people living in Iran. These people travel throughout the country living in certain areas depending on the time of year.

Country Profile: Iran

The Country Profiles Web site from the British Broadcasting Corporation (BBC) contains information on Iran's leaders and media, as well as facts and a basic overview of the country.

EDITOR'S CHOICE

Access this Web site from http://www.myreportlinks.com

2005, Iranian President Mahmoud Ahmadinejad gave a speech in which he said Israel "must be wiped off the map."[3] The country of Israel is the Jewish homeland. It is also located in the Middle East. Fewer than twenty-five thousand Jews remain in postrevolution Iran.[4] Although the people of Iran are from many diverse backgrounds, most have one major thing in common: their religion. About 98 percent of Iranians are followers of Islam. Islam is a religion that began on the Arab peninsula, to the south of Iran, in A.D. 700. Iranians share the Islamic religion with their Arabic neighbors in the Middle East.

Chapter 3

Religion in Iran

The people of ancient Iran had their own gods and goddesses called *daevas*. Some daevas represented the moon, sun, and stars. Other daevas symbolized the elements of nature: fire, earth, water, and air. We know very little for certain about these primitive religions. Over time new religions replaced the ancient ways, and the word *daeva* came to mean "demon."[1]

This Web site from the Iran Chamber Society provides articles dealing with different aspects of cultural and religious beliefs and events.

Access this Web site from http://www.myreportlinks.com

Zoroastrianism

Zoroastrianism is an early religion that began in Iran. It is based on the teachings of a prophet named Zoroaster. Scholars think he lived as early as 1500 B.C.[2] Zoroaster taught his followers to believe in one supreme God. He called this god Ahura Mazda. The idea of only worshipping one all-powerful God was new. People were used to worshiping many different daevas. Zoroaster also spoke about the god's evil twin, Angra Mainyu. Ahura Mazda was light, truth, and goodness. Angra Mainyu was darkness, lies, and evil. Zoroaster said people had a choice: They could follow the path of good or the path of evil. When a person died, Ahura Mazda would judge his life. A good person would live a happy afterlife, while a bad person would suffer. Zoroastrianism was at the center of Iranian culture until the seventh century A.D. Roughly two hundred thousand people around the world still follow the teachings of Zoroaster.

Islam and the Prophet Muhammad

Today, Islam is the leading religion of Iran. Islam is one of the world's fastest-growing major religions. It is based on the teachings of the prophet Muhammad who lived fourteen hundred years ago. Muhammad was born in Mecca, a city in modern-day Saudi Arabia, in A.D. 570. In Muhammad's time, Mecca was the center of Arab civilization. People traveled from all over Arabia to worship at a famous temple there called the Ka'bah. As in ancient Iran, the Arabic tribes then celebrated many different gods. The Ka'bah was a small, cube-shaped building. Inside were hundreds of icons of gods and goddesses.

Muhammad's mother died when he was six, leaving him an orphan. His uncle, a camel caravan leader and trader, took him in. Muhammad learned the merchant trade from his uncle and became a successful business-man. He married a wealthy widow and had a family. It was not until 610, when Muhammad was forty years old, that Allah first spoke to him. *Allah* is the Arabic word meaning "God." The archangel Gabriel came to Muhammad and told him to memorize and spread the

Shi'a Muslims from Iran and Iraq often begin their pilgrimage to Mecca in the Iraqi city of Karbala. Making a pilgrimage to Mecca at least once in a lifetime is one of the Five Pillars of Islam. This image is part of the **BBC News: Middle East** Web site's photo journal.

word of Allah. Learned men wrote down Muhammad's teachings in a holy book called the Qur'an, or Koran.

Muhammad shared Allah's word with the people of Mecca. He preached that people must care for the poor, widowed, and orphaned. Muhammad taught people to stop worshiping the many idols in the Ka'bah. He told them to devote themselves to the one true God. Muhammad also spoke of a final judgment day. When the judgment day comes, Allah will judge each person's life. Muhammad's ideas angered some influential people. Much of Mecca's economy depended on the pilgrimages people made to the Ka'bah.[3]

Muhammad and His Army Spread Islam

In 622, Muhammad and his followers moved to Medina. Medina was a rival trade town located 200 miles to the north. There, Muhammad steadily gained more followers. The people of Medina chose him to be their political leader. Sensing a growing threat as Muhammad's influence grew, Meccans declared war on Medina. Muhammad, now a leader with an army, became a hero when Medina won the war in 630. Mecca, the heart of the Arab world, now became the center of Islam. Muhammad kept the Ka'bah as a holy place, but first he emptied the building and removed all the idols. By the time of his death in 632, Muhammad's religion had been embraced by most of the Arabic world. Arab culture was thriving. Over the next thirty years, the Arab empire grew quickly. Their armies moved to the north and the west, capturing new territory that included modern-day Iran.

When Arabs conquered the area that is now Iran, they brought the religion of Islam with them. Persian culture and Islamic culture melded together in Iran. Today 98 percent of Iranians are Muslim. Muslims are people who practice the religion of Islam. The other 2 percent of Iranians are made up of Zoroastrians, Christians, Jews, and Baha'is. The Baha'i religion is a faith that began in Iran in the 1800s. Americans often make the mistake of assuming that the Muslims of Iran are Arabs.[4] This is not at all true. Only 3 percent of Iranians are ethnic Arabs.

▲ One of the Five Pillars of Islam is that Muslims must pray five times per day while facing Mecca.

Religions of the Middle East

Islam, Christianity, and Judaism are three of the world's major religions. They have much in common. All three religions began in the Middle East and have spread all over the world. Christians, Jews, and Muslims all believe there is only one God, the creator. The city of Jerusalem is holy to all three. They also share some of the same prophets. Muslims regard Abraham, Moses, Jesus, and Muhammad as mortal men who were spoken to by God. Muslims believe that the Old and New Testaments of the Bible are the word of Allah and respect Jesus as one of God's prophets. However, they recognize Muhammad as the most recent and therefore the most important prophet of Allah. The Qur'an is the holy Islamic scripture. While Christians worship Jesus Christ as the son of God, Muslims do not worship the mortal Muhammad. They hold up his life as a model way to live. Muslims highly revere the Qur'an as the word of Allah.[5] Many Muslims memorize parts or all of the Qur'an.

Five Pillars of Islam

The prophet Muhammad set forth five basic duties for Muslims. They are often called the Five Pillars of Islam. The Shahada is the first duty. It is a declaration of faith in Allah. One must say with conviction, "There is no true god but Allah; Muhammad is the messenger of Allah." The second pillar is daily prayer, called Salat. Muslims must pray five times each day: just before sunrise, just after noon, in late afternoon, after sunset, and in the evening. Muslims stand, bow, and kneel often on a

Access this Web site from http://www.myreportlinks.com

Iran's capital city paper, the *Tehran Times*, provides up-to-date news articles on its Web site. Visit its site to read news about Iran and the Middle East.

special prayer mat while reciting portions of the Qur'an. Prayers can be said alone or with groups of other people. If they can, believers are expected on Fridays to attend noontime worship service at the town mosque where the spiritual leader also gives a sermon. Before entering the mosque, people remove their shoes. Then they wash in a fountain or a sink to symbolize the cleansing of their mind. Muslims always face the direction of the Ka'bah in Mecca while praying.

The third pillar is almsgiving. Every year Muslims pay a tax, called zakat. The amount of the tax depends on the amount of one's personal wealth. Religious clerics distribute the money to the poor. Fasting, or going without food and water, is the fourth duty in Islam. Every year during the month of Ramadan, Muslims fast between sunrise and sunset. The Arabic word for this fast is *sawm*. Allah first spoke to Muhammad during the month of Ramadan. Ramadan is the ninth month of the Islamic year. Muslims follow a lunar calendar based on the phases of the moon. There are twelve lunar months each year. Each month is twenty-nine or thirty days long.

The Pilgrimage

The final pillar of Islam is the hajj, or a pilgrimage to Mecca. Every Muslim who is financially and physically able must complete a hajj during his or her lifetime. The hajj is a five-day journey. It occurs every year, beginning on the eighth day of Dhul-Hijjah, the last of the twelve lunar months. The hajj is a huge event, drawing millions of Muslims from all over the world to the deserts of Saudi Arabia. One American Muslim, describing the importance of her hajj, wrote "Hajj is considered partly a rehearsal for the Day of Judgement."[6]

The pilgrims, or hajjis, purify themselves by washing and wearing special clothes. The women wear loose, ankle-length dresses. Men wrap two white cloths around themselves. Throughout their journey they recite words that tell Allah they are responding to his call. Once in Mecca, the hajjis walk seven times around the ancient Ka'bah. The Ka'bah is draped with a black cloth inscribed with verses from the Qur'an. Next they drink holy water from the ancient Zamzam well. The following day is the day of Arafat. The hajjis gather at a mosque 12 miles southeast of Mecca. It is the site of Muhammad's last

▲ *People in both traditional dress and Western clothes gather in the courtyard of the Shrine of Hazrat Fatimeh, in Iran.*

sermon. They spend the entire day in prayer, asking Allah to forgive their sins. That night they stay in tents in the valley of Muzdalifah, praying and gathering small stones. The next morning they travel to Mena, a few miles to the east of Mecca. During the day the pilgrims throw stones at ancient pillars called the Jamarats. The pillars mark the spots where Satan appeared to the prophet Abraham. After the first day of stoning, the men shave the hair from their heads. Women often simply clip a lock of hair.

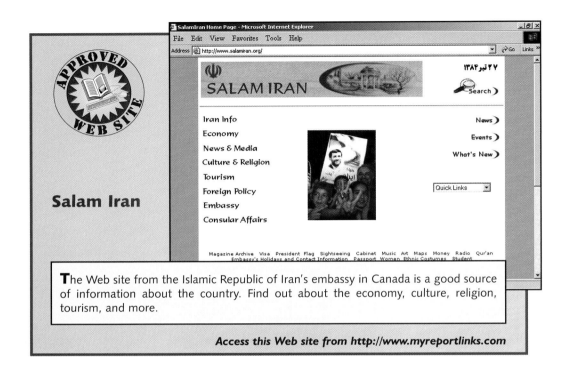

The Web site from the Islamic Republic of Iran's embassy in Canada is a good source of information about the country. Find out about the economy, culture, religion, tourism, and more.

Access this Web site from http://www.myreportlinks.com

A pilgrim's hajj is complete after walking seven final circles around the Ka'bah.

Shi'a and Sunni Muslims

Although most Iranians are Muslim, they do not all belong to the same sect, or group, of Islam. The majority of Muslims worldwide belong to the Sunni sect. Iran, however, is one country where the Shi'a Muslims are in the majority. The division between these two groups began when the prophet Muhammad died. He died before appointing a successor to lead the Muslim people. A council of Muslim leaders met to elect the new leader called a caliph. They chose a man named Abu Bakr who had worked closely with Muhammad. Not all Muslims were happy with this decision. Some felt the successor should have been Muhammad's cousin and son-in-law, a man named 'Ali ibn Abi Talib. Sunni Muslims believe in the system of electing caliphs. The Shi'a Muslims feel only 'Ali's descendants have the right to lead the Muslim community.

► Baha'i

A small minority of Iranians follow the fledgling Baha'i faith. Like Zoroastrianism, Baha'i is a religion that began in Persia. The Baha'i prophet was a man from Tehran named Mirza Husayn 'Ali. He lived from 1817 to 1892. His followers call him Baha'u'llah, meaning "Glory of God." The shah refused to recognize this new religion and sent the prophet into exile. The Baha'i religion grew out of Shia Islam and has many similarities. The Baha'i pray daily and fast for nineteen days of the year. There are also clear differences between Islam and the Baha'i faith. The Baha'i have no clergy, or people with religious authority. They believe in equal treatment and opportunities for men and women. The main goal of the Baha'i is to bring the people of the world together in peace. Although Iran is the birthplace of their faith, the Baha'i have never been accepted there. They continue to be persecuted for practicing their religion.

► Islamic Republic of Iran

In the 1970s, many Iranians lived in poverty and fear. The shah and his cohorts hoarded great wealth. They did not allow anyone to speak against them. In 1979, the people of Iran worked together to overthrow the shah. When the government toppled, Iran was in a state of

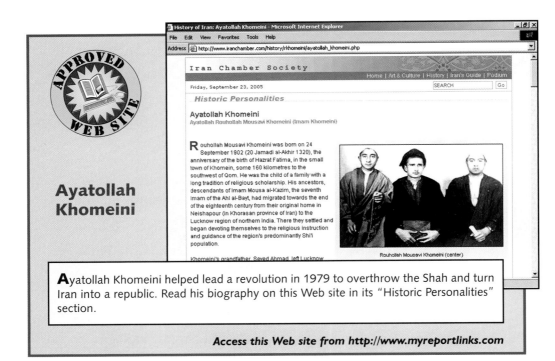

Ayatollah Khomeini

Ayatollah Khomeini helped lead a revolution in 1979 to overthrow the Shah and turn Iran into a republic. Read his biography on this Web site in its "Historic Personalities" section.

Access this Web site from http://www.myreportlinks.com

chaos. The man who led the opposition to the shah was the Ayatollah Ruholla Khomeini. The Persian word *ayatollah* is a religious title. Under the ayatollah's leadership, they renamed their country the Islamic Republic of Iran. The ayatollah and his supporters hoped to recreate the glory of Muhammad's time. In those long-ago days of the Arab empire, Islamic culture had been a powerful and prosperous world force. With this in mind, Iran developed a new constitution, or set of laws defining the government. The new laws were based on the teachings of the holy Qur'an. This was in keeping with Muslim tradition. For example, Muhammad himself had been a political leader. Muhammad had also founded his government on the word of Allah.

Iran vs. the West

For several reasons, the new government of Iran saw the West as an enemy. The West, or the nations of Europe and the Americas, are powerful military and economic forces in the world today. The ayatollah declared the United States in particular a threat to the young nation. The religious differences between the two countries were part of the problem. The United States feels that Iran's theocratic regime is undemocratic. The U.S. Constitution states that religion and government must be independent from one another. Iran's constitution is founded on Islam. Church and state stand together.

Also, many Iranians distrust America because of what happened in 1953. The United States Central Intelligence Agency (CIA) led a coup that forced the government of Mohammed Mossadegh out of office. They reinstalled Shah Mohammad Reza Pahlavi. Since then, Iranians have feared that the United States would interfere with their government once again.

Chapter 4

Iranian Art and Culture

Persia is famous the world over for its handmade carpets, often called Persian rugs. Tribal animal herders created the first knotted rugs. They wove yarn made from the coats of sheep and goats. Warm rugs insulated and decorated the floors and walls of their tents. Persian

▲ Persian carpets made in Iran are known around the world for their beauty and quality.

carpets were at their glory in the sixteenth century. Persia exported the colorful, intricate rugs to Europeans, who highly prized them. Persian carpets often depict plants and gardens. Others picture court life, hunting, or battle scenes. Some rug makers weave complicated, geometric designs.

▶ The Written Word

It is difficult for Americans to imagine the role that poetry plays in Iran. Poetry holds a special place in the hearts of Iranians. All Iranians can recite lines from famous

▲ *The Qur'an is the most important book in Iranian culture, and the holy book of Islam.*

Persian poems. Perhaps the most famous poem in Iran is *Shahnamah,* or *The Epic of Kings,* by Firdawsi. It is a book-length, epic poem. Written in the tenth century A.D., the poem captured and preserved stories from Persia's past. Iranians love poetry not only for its beauty, but also because it has played an important role in Persia's long history. When Persia was under foreign control, poets kept the Persian language and culture alive. Another influential poet was Hafez. His name means "one who memorizes." Hafez lived in the city of Shiraz in the 1300s. He wrote poems about love, wine, and nightingales.

Writing, Architecture, and Music

Calligraphy is the art of fine penmanship. The Qur'an forbids people to represent people and animals in art. Islamic artists turned their skill to writing. Examples of calligraphy are everywhere in Iran. The national flag, for example, features a stylized tulip. The tulip is actually the word "Allah," or "God," written in calligraphy. Calligraphy finds beauty in written words. It celebrates the Muslim saying "Allah is beautiful and loves beauty." Words from the Qur'an often decorate the walls of mosques. Persian architecture is known for its simple elegance. Iran's dramatic natural landscape enhances the splendor of many mosques and palaces. Since the arrival of Islam, Persians reserved Iran's best architecture for mosques. Iran's mosques are famous for their tiles. The vivid-colored tiles decorate the holy buildings both inside and out.

▲ Mosques throughout the Middle East represent the best architecture in the Islamic world. This shrine is located in Qom, Iran.

Traditional Iranian music is poetry sung to music. Iranian musicians use many eastern instruments that are unfamiliar in the West. The *tar* is a six-stringed instrument. It has a long, thin neck. It is plucked, like a guitar. The *nay* is a reed flute. The musician holds it vertically, like a recorder. A *tombak* is a drum carved out of a single piece of wood. The drumhead is made from a tightly stretched sheepskin membrane. A *kamanche* is a type of violin with four strings. The Islamic Republic censors any music that it deems un-Islamic. This includes most pop music. Radios and televisions broadcast a constant signal of people chanting the Qur'an. The chant sounds very musical, though instruments do not accompany it.

Persian Food

Persian cuisine draws on locally grown food and spices. Iranians use vegetables such as cauliflower, eggplant, tomatoes, spinach, beans, lentils, and onions. Garlic, turmeric, mint, parsley, coriander, cardamom, marjoram, and saffron add color and spice. Pistachios, hazelnuts, and walnuts contribute a healthy crunch to their diet. Iranians eat their largest meal of the day at lunchtime. A Persian lunch usually includes a rice dish. Iranians enjoy fruit for dessert. Apples, dates, peaches, citrus, melons, and pomegranates are local and delicious. Alcohol is against Islamic law, and is not served in Iran, although it can be found illegally. The Qur'an also forbids pork. Iranians eat lamb, mutton (sheep), chicken, and beef. All meat must come from animals slaughtered according

**Vis à Vis:
Beyond
the Veil**

The *Beyond the Veil* Web site from PBS contains information about women in Iran, the Islamic revolution, Iranian culture, and more. It also has two women, one from Iran and the other from the United States. They compare their upbringing and they share their views of one another.

Access this Web site from http://www.myreportlinks.com

to religious law. Tea and coffee are popular drinks. Iranians gather at teahouses to unwind and chat with their neighbors. Tea drinkers hold a cube of sugar behind their teeth. They sip tea through the sugar cube. Coffee is thick and sweet.

▶ Ta'arof—The Art of Respectful Conversation

Polite conversation is an art form. When we are polite, we communicate respect. Yet what is polite in one country may be impolite in another. Iranians have a traditional way of speaking politely to one another. This custom is called ta'arof. *Ta'arof* means "courtly phrases" in Farsi. Outsiders unfamiliar with this custom may be baffled. Even worse, they may be offended or misunderstood.

Here is a common example of ta'arof. An Iranian may offer a visitor a generous gift. According to Persian tradition, the guest refuses the gift. The offer of the gift is a sign of respect. The guest feels flattered, but would never dream of accepting. Americans, however, are used to speaking in a more forthright manner. In the United States, it would be polite to take the gift.

Iranian customs sometimes offend Westerners as well. In Iran it is common to ask questions about a person's salary or marital status. To Westerners these subjects feel too private to discuss with strangers.[1] Ta'arof also includes polite small talk. It is customary to talk about family and health at the start of a new conversation.

A Girl's Life

Being female in Iran is quite different from being female in America. Iran has strict laws about what females over the age of nine may wear in public. These laws come from the Qur'an and Islamic traditions. Women are required to wear a loose-fitting robe called a chador at all religious sites. The chador completely covers a woman's body from head to toe. Chadors were made mandatory in 1981, but it is common to see a woman wear a long-sleeved, knee-length coat called a manteau, or other long coat instead. Under the manteau, she wears pants. Thick socks cover her ankles. A *maghnae,* or scarf, veils her head and shoulders. None of her hair should show. Makeup is not allowed. This dress code is called *hejab.* Few women dare to appear in public without following

▲ *These women exiting the Tomb of Imam Reza in Mashhad, Iran, are wearing traditional chadors.*

FRONTLINE/WORLD . Iran - Forbidden Iran . Interview With Iranian Nobel Prize Winner Shirin Ebad - Microsoft Internet Explorer

File   Edit   View   Favorites   Tools   Help

Address   http://www.pbs.org/frontlineworld/stories/iran/ebadi.html

PBS HOME   PROGRAMS A-Z   TV SCHEDULES   SUPPORT PBS   SHOP PBS   SEARCH PBS

FRONTLINE
WORLD

SEARCH WORLD

Home   Stories   React   About FRONTLINE/World   Recent Posts   Educators   FRONTLINE

IRAN - Forbidden Iran, January 2004

RELATED FEATURES

THE STORY
Synopsis of "Forbidden
Iran"

THE STRUGGLE FOR
DEMOCRACY
A Brief History

INTERVIEW WITH JANE
KOKAN
Undercover With the
Underground

INTERVIEW WITH SHIRIN
EBADI

Interview With Iranian Nobel Prize Winner Shirin Ebadi

Shirin Ebadi, age 56, has fought for women's rights, children's rights and human rights for years, defending political activists and other human rights lawyers. Ebadi was Iran's first woman judge before the 1979 Islamic rev — at which point she was the mullahs. As a lawyer part-time lecturer at Teh University, she has argu there is no contradiction Islam and human rights. been previously jailed for h defense of political activists

Shirin Ebadi featured in a
FRONTLINE/World interview Nov.
2003.

APPROVED WEB SITE

Shirin Ebadi has been active in the struggle for women's rights in Iran. As a lawyer, she is representing Zahra Kazemi, a Canadian journalist who was murdered in Iran. Read this article at the **Iran: Forbidden Iran** Web page, part of the PBS series *Frontline*.

the hejab. The punishment is a lashing, although it is not enforced consistently.

In the 1980s and 1990s, groups of police roamed the streets in white Toyotas. They looked for women not obeying the hejab laws. To Americans, these laws are shocking. In a country where the heat can be oppressive, these layers of clothes seem cruel. Some Iranian women feel more comfortable dressed this way. Some women chose to dress this way even before it became a law due to their religious beliefs. Other Iranian women seem to be growing tired of these strict laws. In Tehran today, some women are wearing fashionable fitted,

Number 2327
Tue, Jul 19, 2005
Tir 28 1384
jamadi'ol sani 12 1426

IRAN ● DAILY

Advanced Search

PDF
Version

Front Page
National
Domestic Economy
Science
Panorama
Economic Focus
Dot Coms
Global Energy
World Politics
Sports

Iran Daily

Iran Favors Independent, United Iraq
President-Elect Calls for Closer Cooperation

Abadan-Basra Oil Pipeline Under Construction

TEHRAN, July 18--Leader of the Islamic Revolution Ayatollah Seyyed Ali Khamenei said on Monday an independent and unified Iraq, which is secure and tranquil, is a top priority of Iran.
Ayatollah Khamenei, who received Iraqi Prime Minister Ibrahim Jaafari in Mashhad, added, "The Iraqi nation is the true brother of the Iranian nation. The people of Iraq hated the measures adopted by the former Baathist regime during the Iraq-imposed war (1980-88). The ouster of Saddam Hussein was good news for both the people of Iraq and Iran."
The leader noted that enemies

This Web site provides daily news stories about Iran and the rest of the world. Visit it now to see the current news.

Access this Web site from http://www.myreportlinks.com

bright-colored coats instead of the drab, loose-fitting traditional ones. Some wear makeup or let some of their hair show under their veils. However, the hejab laws are still on the books. It remains to be seen whether police will crack down on these rule breakers.

Iran's constitution says women are mothers and homemakers, whose realm is the home. Yet many middle-class women also work jobs outside of the home. Their families need the additional money. First, women must gain permission to work from the male head of the household. Women and men stay apart from each other in many parts of society. The government segregates schools by gender. This means that girls and boys study separately.

At the university level, there are some subjects that women are not allowed to study. On city buses, women and men sit apart. A woman may not appear in public with a man, unless he is her husband or a family member. Despite all these limits, Iranian women are often better off than their sisters in other Middle Eastern countries. Unlike nearby Saudi Arabia, Iranian women can drive a car and vote. When women gained the right to vote in 1963, Iranian conservatives held large protests. Still, women kept this right after the revolution. Women hold positions in the parliament. Women have regained some rights since the death of the Ayatollah Khomeini in 1989.

Polygamy, defined as marrying more than one wife, is legal in Iran. Men can marry up to four wives. Under the last shah, the legal marrying age was eighteen. After the revolution, marriage law changed. Men could legally marry girls as young as nine years old. This law was based on the life of the prophet Muhammad. He married his favorite wife when she was nine. Once a girl is married, she can no longer attend high school. In recent years, reformists pushed to have this law changed. Now the legal marrying age for girls is thirteen. Boys may marry at age fifteen—the same age all Iranians gain the right to vote.

▷ Celebrating the Persian New Year

Norouz, or the Persian New Year, is a festive time in Iran. It is a national holiday, and the biggest celebration of the entire year. Norouz begins on the first day of spring and lasts for two weeks. For days in advance, families prepare to welcome in the new year by giving their houses a thorough spring-cleaning. On the last night of the old year, people light bonfires and sing songs. This evening celebration is *Chahar Shanbeh Soori,* or the festival of fires. It is a tradition to jump over the fires. While they jump, they sing "Give me your beautiful red color and take back my sickly pallor!"[2] These customs date back to three thousand years ago, when ancient Zoroastrians used fire in their worship rituals. Iranians believe wishes will come true on this night. It is traditional to eat a mix of dried fruit and nuts. Children put disguises on and go door to door asking for treats. The day seems a lot like Halloween in the United States.

▶ A Festive Day

When the first day of spring arrives, families spend the day together and exchange gifts. The women prepare huge feasts, including a traditional rice dish. Mothers eat hard-boiled eggs, one for each of their children. According to Persian ritual, the table is set with seven items. Each begins with the letter s in Farsi. They often include apples (*sib*), green grass (*sabze*), vinegar (*serkeh*), berries (*senjed*), ground wheat (*samanoo*), a gold coin (*sekke*), and garlic (*sir*). A bowl of goldfish usually decorates the table. Most families add the Qur'an and a poetry book by one of Iran's popular poets, Hafez or Firdawsi.[3] Iranians spend the first two weeks of the new year visiting with family. The thirteenth day of the New Year is called Sizdah-Bedar. Iranians consider the thirteenth day to be bad luck. To avoid the bad luck, they leave their homes and head outside. Parks are full of people picnicking and playing.

Sports in Iran

Iranians are fiercely proud of their soccer team. Iran competes internationally. Top Iranian players are drafted to play in the European soccer leagues. Soccer stadiums are for men only. In 1998, Iran's soccer team played well in the World Cup. Iranians were excited to see their country excel in an international forum. That year, Iran formed a women's team. The women may only play indoors, and no men are allowed to watch. Iran has an excellent men's wrestling team. The world-famous team has won Olympic medals.

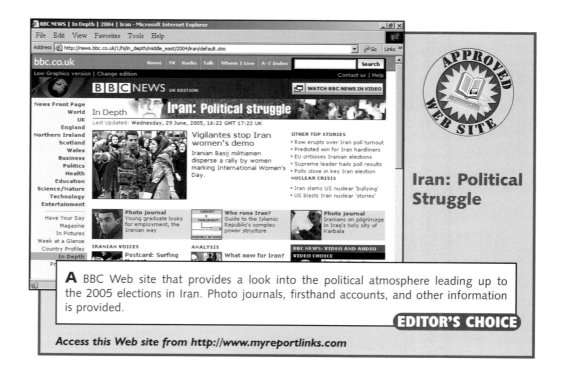

Iran: Political Struggle

A BBC Web site that provides a look into the political atmosphere leading up to the 2005 elections in Iran. Photo journals, firsthand accounts, and other information is provided.

EDITOR'S CHOICE

Access this Web site from http://www.myreportlinks.com

American Influence—Keeping the "Great Satan" Out

As children, Iranians learn to chant "Death to America!" at school.[4] Religious leaders echo this anti-American propaganda during Friday prayers. Government officials routinely refer to the United States as "the Great Satan." Yet American visitors to Iran report that Iranians are welcoming and courteous. Iranians take pride in treating guests with great respect. They may oppose the actions of the United States government, but they are friendly to individual Americans. Many young Iranians really admire American culture, music, and social freedoms.[5]

▲ A student at Azad University uses a computer at an Internet cafe to complete a project. Internet cafes began to open in Iran in 1999.

The Islamic Republic tries to keep America out of Iran. Yet many people seek out American culture. They have satellite television, broadband radios, or the Internet.

In 2004, 7 million, or one out of every ten Iranians had access to the Internet.[6] The government can ban the printing of a newspaper, but it has a more difficult time controlling the Internet. It can close down Web sites, but it cannot stop the same information from reappearing at a different Web address. Satellite television is illegal, but police do not strictly enforce these laws. The year 2004 brought renewed crackdowns on journalists. Police are arresting people for posting their views on the Internet. Human rights organizations say Iran uses torture and imprisonment to quiet government critics. A worker for the nonprofit Human Rights Watch noted "Iran is sending a message to its critics: keep silent or face years in prison."[7] Tired of the social and economic problems, nearly two hundred thousand Iranians move to a different country each year.[8]

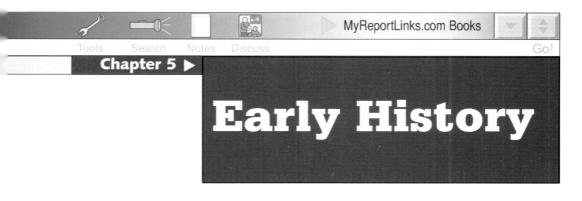

Chapter 5

Early History

People have lived in Iran since prehistoric times. Prehistory was the time before people developed a system of writing. The earliest cultures left no written history. Thanks to archaeology, we know a little about Iran's prehistoric people. Archaeologists are scientists

This ancient cup shows four gazelles walking. More artifacts like this can be viewed at the **Timeline of Art History: Iran** Web page, part of the Metropolitan Museum of Art.

who uncover objects from the past. It takes something sturdy to survive for thousands of years. Some common objects archaeologists find are tools, pottery, arrowheads, jewelry, bones, and teeth. Using these clues, archaeologists try to solve the mystery of what life was like long ago.

Iran once had a very different climate than it does today. Over fifteen thousand years ago, Iran had more forests, lakes, and streams. People hunted animals and gathered wild plants. They made their homes in mountain caves. As the climate grew drier, people had to adapt. They began to cultivate plants. They burned forests to make more fields. They discovered that stones and metals could be used for building materials, jewelry, and tools. Early people used copper, lead, gold, silver, lapis lazuli, and iron.[1]

▷ Elamites and the Mysterious Ziggurat

At Choga Zanbil in western Iran, people can view a man-made mountain of ancient brick. It is a ziggurat, a temple in the shape of a pyramid tower. The Elamites, who lived here as early as 2700 B.C., built the ziggurat over three thousand years ago. Elamites were the first Iranians to leave behind written records. Their records tell stories of battles and merchant trade with their neighbors, the kingdoms of Assyria, Babylonia, and Sumer. In 644 B.C., Assyrian armies from present-day Iraq marched into Elam. The soldiers demolished Elam's capital city, Susa. Elamite civilization came to an end.[2]

Iran, 8000–2000 B.C.

Enlarge Description

Head of a ruler, ca. 2300–2000 B.C.
Iran or Mesopotamia
Arsenical copper; H. 13 1/2 in. (34.3 cm)
Rogers Fund, 1947 (47.100.80)

The **Timeline of Art History: Iran** Web site from the Metropolitan Museum of Art has a lot of great photos and information about the ancient peoples who lived in what is now Iran.

▷ The Achaemenids and the First Great Persian Empire

With Elamite civilization in ruins, newcomer Aryan tribes took charge. They had come from the steppes, or grass-lands, of southeastern Europe. The Aryans were talented horse and cattle breeders. They were also skilled metal-workers who made tools and art from bronze. Two main tribes of Aryan people settled in Iran: the Medes and the Persians. The Medes came first, building villages in Iran by 900 B.C. Their capital was Ecbatana, at the site of the modern Iranian city Hamadan. The Magi, a group of

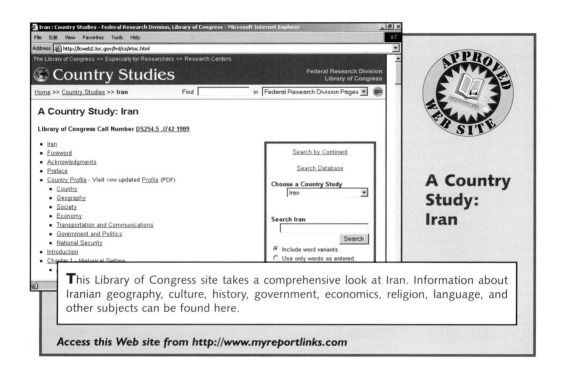

A Country Study: Iran

Iran : Country Studies - Federal Research Division, Library of Congress - Microsoft Internet Explorer

File Edit View Favorites Tools Help

Address http://lcweb2.loc.gov/frd/cs/irtoc.html

The Library of Congress >> Especially for Researchers >> Research Centers

Country Studies

Federal Research Division
Library of Congress

Home >> Country Studies >> Iran   Find   in Federal Research Division Pages go

A Country Study: Iran

Library of Congress Call Number DS254.5 .I742 1989

- Iran
- Foreword
- Acknowledgments
- Preface
- Country Profile - Visit new updated Profile (PDF)
  - Country
  - Geography
  - Society
  - Economy
  - Transportation and Communications
  - Government and Politics
  - National Security
- Introduction
- Chapter 1 - Historical Setting

Search by Continent

Search Database

Choose a Country Study
Iran

Search Iran

Search

⦿ Include word variants .
○ Use only words as entered.

This Library of Congress site takes a comprehensive look at Iran. Information about Iranian geography, culture, history, government, economics, religion, language, and other subjects can be found here.

Access this Web site from http://www.myreportlinks.com

powerful sorcerer-priests, ruled the Medes. The word magic derives from their religious ceremonies. After the Assyrians destroyed Elam, the Medes realized they would need help to avoid a similar fate. Joining forces with the Babylonians, they defeated the powerful Assyrian Empire. The Medes then controlled Iran. Their territory included that of their fellow Aryans, the Persians. Persians had settled in the Zagros Mountains, near modern-day Shiraz.

It was the Persians, not the Medes, who would take control of Iran and turn it into a world power. In 559 B.C., Persian leader Cyrus the Great led a successful revolt against the Median king. Thus began the first Persian Empire, called the Achaemenid dynasty. Cyrus did not stop when he conquered the Medes. At the height of power, the Achaemenids ruled the entire Middle East and parts of Central Asia. Cyrus built a new capital city in his homeland, high in the Zagros Mountains. The city was called Pasargadae. The architecture of the buildings reflected the many cultures under Persian rule. Cyrus was a tolerant leader. He let people continue to worship their traditional gods. When Cyrus captured the city of Babylon, he released forty thousand Jewish slaves. He allowed them to return to Palestine and rebuild their temple. As a result of his kind leadership, Cyrus was remembered as a just king.[3]

▲ *Persepolis was the capital city of the Persian Empire ruled by Darius the Great. Each year many people travel to see the ruins of this important ancient city.*

These Muslim pilgrims are visiting the Tomb of Imam Reza in Mashhad, Iran. Mashhad was a stop along the Great Silk Road, an ancient route of travel that brought prosperity to the region.

Cyrus the Great died on the battlefield. Even at the end of his life, he was fighting to expand his empire. One of his sons, Cambyses II, became leader. Cambyses attacked and took over Egypt during his short reign. He died on his way back to Persia from Egypt. A distant relative named Darius I gained the throne and ruled for over thirty years. Darius strengthened the Persian Empire, which now included 50 million people. Darius set up a monetary system based on gold and silver coins. He made laws, built roads, and established taxes. He ordered a canal to be built from the Nile River to the Red Sea. Darius governed his empire by splitting it into regions. He put leaders, called satraps, in charge of the regions. The satraps reported directly to him. Darius built grand palaces at a new capital city called Persepolis. Persepolis is 30 miles from Cyrus' Pasargadae. Ruins of both these magnificent cities still remain.

When Darius died, King Xerxes took power and ruled from 486–465 B.C. Under his rule the Persians and Greeks entered into war. This war would eventually be fatal to the Persian Empire. One hundred and fifty years later, Alexander the Great, king of Macedonia, defeated Greece. He then turned to the Persian Empire. He fought his way through Egypt, Turkey, and Iraq. His armies destroyed the Persians in their own homeland in 331 B.C. The first Persian Empire had come to an end. Alexander burned Persepolis, but not before dragging off as much treasure as possible. Alexander continued to expand his rule to the east, as far as India.

► Iran in Medieval Times

When Alexander died, his generals divided his huge empire into three parts. Iran fell under the rule of the Seleucids. The Seleucids were strongly influenced by Greek culture. For nearly one hundred years, Persia was part of this foreign empire. Then, in 238 B.C., a group of tribes banded together to overthrow the Seleucids. The tribes, called the Parthians, came from Eastern Iran. They lived between the Caspian and the Aral seas. The Parthians ruled Iran until third century A.D. They were expert horsemen and archers. They were not very good record keepers, however. If they had any written records, none have survived. The little we know about the Parthians comes from the writings of their enemies, the Romans.

The Sassanians Rebuild the Persian Empire

While the Parthian armies were busy fighting the Romans, all was not quiet at home in Iran. Back in the Zagros Mountains, the Persians were growing tired of Parthian rule. Led by Ardeshir of the Sassanian family, the Persians challenged the Parthians in A.D. 224. The Persians won easily. Protecting the country from the Romans had severely weakened the Parthian armies. Ardeshir named his quickly growing nation the Sassanian Empire. The Sassanid kings saw themselves as part of a line of Persian nobles. They prided themselves on being Persian kings in the tradition of Cyrus the Great and Darius. They declared the old Persian religion of Zoroastrianism to be the new state religion. Perhaps in reaction to years of foreign occupation, the Sassanid kings did not tolerate the worship of other gods. The Sassanids ruled until the seventh century A.D. Then Arabs invaded, and Persia was under foreign rule yet again.

Persians Embrace Islam

Within one hundred years of the death of the Prophet Muhammad, Islam had spread rapidly and widely. People from Persia, Egypt, Morocco, China, Indonesia, Spain,

▲ *Beginning around A.D. 650, Iran started to become an Islamic region. Today, mosques are everywhere in Iran. This one is in the center of the city of Tehran.*

and Russia had adopted the Muslim faith. Each Muslim had a sacred duty to spread the word of Allah. In 642, just ten years after the prophet's death, Arabs fought the Persians at the Battle of Nehavand. The Iranian town of Nehavand stood between the Muslim armies and a mountain pass that led into central Iran. When Persia lost the battle, the empire never recovered. In 651, the last Sassanian king, Yazdegerd, was murdered by one of his own people. The second rising of the Persian Empire fell to Arab rule.

Iran gradually became an Islamic country. The old Persian ways and the new Islamic religion melded together to form a new Persian culture. In the eighth century, Iranians began to revolt against the Arab rulers. Eventually they broke away altogether and local leaders took charge. The Samanids of eastern Iran ruled the country from A.D. 819 to 1005. They revived the written Persian language. The Iranian Samanids were Muslim, but they were also proud of their Persian heritage.[4] The Samanids made a big mistake when they built their armies with Turkish slaves. The Samanids were destroyed by their own armies. Turks then controlled Iran until the thirteenth century. Persian art, science, and poetry blossomed under Turkish rule.

▶ Violence and Greed of the Mongol Invaders

Under the leadership of the legendary warrior Genghis Khan, Mongols invaded eastern Iran in 1219. The Mongols were tribal people from central Asia. Unlike Turks and Persians, the Mongols did not practice Islam. The Mongol era was an extremely violent time in Persian history. Their armies looted Persian cities and ruined farmlands. They destroyed local architecture and art. Worst of all, they killed entire cities of people.[5] The Mongols controlled Persia until the fifteenth century. Timur was the last of the Mongol leaders. He was a ruthless, Turkish-speaking Mongol warrior who claimed to be related to Genghis Khan. Timur fought a series of

▲ The Shah-En-Shah monument was erected in 1971 to celebrate the 2,500th anniversary of the Persian Empire. The name has since been changed to the Azadi Monument, which means "freedom" in the Farsi language.

battles in Iran from 1380 until 1393. He united the country under one empire, instead of many regional Mongol leaders. Timur conquered much of Central Asia and the Middle East. After his death, his empire quickly fell apart.

Shi'ism in Iran

In 1501, the Safavids gained control of Iran. Safavids were Turkish-speaking Muslims from west of the Caspian Sea. They claimed to be descended from the prophet Muhammad. This appealed to many Persians. They saw the Safavids as their rightful political and religious leaders. The Safavids made the Shi'a sect of Islam the state religion, as it remains today. Under Safavid rule, religious leaders called mojtaheds gained great power. The mojtaheds became the only ones qualified to interpret Muslim law.

Shah Abbas was the most influential of the Safavid rulers. He governed from 1587 to 1629. Abbas was a patron of the arts. He built a glorious capital city at Isfahan. Today, Isfahan, with its beautiful architecture, is called the jewel of the Muslim world. Abbas was the first shah to enter into diplomatic talks with modern European powers. In 1507, the Portuguese occupied the island of Hormuz in the Persian Gulf. Shah Abbas gave the British trading rights with Persia. In return, the British helped to oust the Portuguese. With the death of Shah Abbas, the Safavid Empire quickly declined. When an Afghani tribe attacked eastern Iran in 1732, the Safavids were in no shape to fight back.

As the Safavid dynasty fell to pieces, a powerful military man named Nader Khan Afshar emerged. Nader rid Persia of the invading Afghanis. Thankful Persians crowned Nader Shah in 1736. Nader tried to expand the empire east into India. He raised taxes to fund his unpopular military adventures. Nader grew obsessed with the idea that people were plotting to overthrow him. He may have been right. In 1747, his top advisors had him murdered in his sleep. Two tribes, the Zands and Qajars, now fought for control of Persia. By 1763, the Persian Zands controlled most of Iran, but it was not to last. In 1797, the Azari Qajars took charge. They moved the capital to Tehran, where they ruled into the twentieth century.

On the CNN Web site, you can read the top news stories from the Middle East, including Iran.

Access this Web site from http://www.myreportlinks.com

Europe Takes an Interest

With the country united once again, Persia now turned its focus to foreign threats. In 1804, the Russians attacked Azerbaijan, then a part of Persia. When Persia turned to its British allies, they refused to help. Russia and Persia resolved the war in 1813 with the Treaty of Golestan. Peace was short lived. In 1826, Persia attacked Russia. Religious differences between Christian Russia and Muslim Persia fueled passions. Despite signing a treaty with Iran in 1814, the British once again refused to aid Persia. When Russia and Persia signed the Treaty of Turkmenchai in 1828, Persia lost all the disputed land. The Persian government was forced to pay lots of money to Russia in war reparations.

In 1856, Persia grew concerned about the British presence in the Middle East. Persia attacked Herat, in British-controlled Afghanistan in 1856. British troops counterattacked from the Persian Gulf. The two countries signed the Treaty of Paris the following year. Iran gave up all claims to Afghanistan. The British and Russians continued to gain power in the region, while Persia lost ground. Persia desperately needed to modernize so it could compete with these new powers. Nasser al-Din Shah attempted to improve banking, mining, and transportation. He hired foreign companies, mostly British, to bring Persia into the modern world.

Tobacco Rebellions of 1891–1892

Persia was left weak and poor after years of fighting. Desperate for money, the shah granted the British

Imperial Tobacco Corporation sole rights to produce, sell, and import tobacco in Persia for the next fifty years. In return, the British gave the shah spending money to finance his extravagant lifestyle. Persians were outraged. Protests broke out in many cities. Religious leaders issued a holy decree, called a *fatwa,* banning the use of tobacco. The entire country boycotted tobacco. The shah was forced to cancel his agreement with the British.

Chapter 6

Modern History

As the twentieth century began, Persians were restless. The success of the Tobacco Rebellion stirred up more calls for change. Persians had seen that when they spoke as one, their voice was strong. The shah had been forced to listen to their needs. In 1906, Persia adopted a new constitution. The constitution was a document that

▲ Russian soldiers perform a military drill in Persia around the time of World War I.

limited the powers of the shah. It established the Majles, or national parliament. Persians now had a voice in their government. In 1909, Mozafaredin Shah was removed from power and his son, Ahmad Mirza, took the throne. At first the new shah agreed to uphold the constitution. Before long he had changed his mind. He backed out of some of his promises. When people protested, the shah called out the army to quiet them.

During World War I, Russian and British forces split Persia between them. The Persians were unhappy, but there was little they could do. Russia had charge of the north, while the British occupied the south. In 1917, there was a revolution in Russia. Russia became part of the USSR: the Union of Soviet Socialist Republics. In 1920, some people of Iran's Gilan province, who were influenced by the Soviet's socialist ideas, decided to break away from Persia. Gilan is a part of Iran that borders the Caspian Sea. Gilan wanted to join the new Soviet Republics. When the shah did not react, the British stepped in. Great Britain did not want their Soviet foes to gain too much power. The British supported the Persian Army, led by military commander Reza Khan. Reza Khan retook Gilan province. With that accomplished, he marched on Tehran and overthrew the last Qajar shah.

Reza Khan and the Pahlavi Dynasty

In 1925, Reza Khan took the throne and changed his name to Reza Shah Pahlavi, but he is commonly referred to as the Reza Shah. His coronation ceremony was a lavish affair. It took place at the opulent Golestan palace in Tehran. The new shah wore a crown made just for the occasion. It was decorated with over three thousand diamonds. Reza Shah quickly set to work modernizing Persia. He did not depend too heavily on the U.S.S.R. or Great Britain. He developed economic ties with Germany, France, and Italy. The ambitious shah made many improvements. He built roads, established industry, and improved health care and public education.[1] He sent Iranian students to schools in Europe. In 1935, he changed the country's name to Iran. In 1936, Reza Shah made it illegal for women to appear in public wearing

▲ *The U.S.S.R. occupied Tehran during World War II in 1941. In this photo, Soviet soldiers are using Tehran as a training ground for launching an attack in Europe.*

the veil. This went against the Qur'an. It angered many Iranians. They wanted to be free to practice their religion.

During World War II, Nazi Germany attacked the Soviet Union. Now the British and Soviets were allied against Germany, their common enemy. Officially, Iran did not take sides in World War II. However, Reza Shah was on friendly terms with the Germans. The British wanted to use Iran's railroads. They would bring troops and supplies from the Persian Gulf to the Soviet Union. Allied forces entered Iran and removed Reza Shah from the throne. Reza Shah's son, Mohammad Reza Pahlavi, took power in 1942. By 1946, the war was over and all foreign troops had withdrawn. Iran was independent once again.

▶ Oil and the Battle for Independence

In the late 1940s, Iranians began protesting foreign control of Iran's oil. Oil was the country's biggest asset. The Qajar shahs had sold the rights to Iran's oil to the British. The Anglo-Iranian Oil Company still controlled Iran's oil fields. Oil was plentiful and in high demand. The British pocketed huge profits. Dr. Mohammed Mossadegh was a lawyer from Iran. He vowed to take back Iran's oil fields from the British. His ideas gained popular support. Anti-British sentiment was widespread in Iran. The shah appointed Mossadegh to be the new prime minister. Mossadegh made good on his word. He kicked out the British and put the oil industry under the Iranian government's charge. The outraged British boycotted Iran's oil.

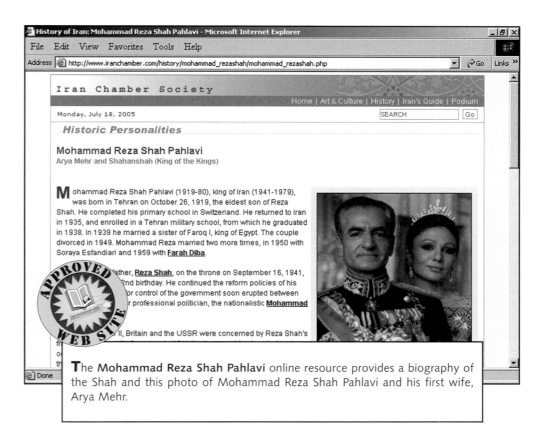

The **Mohammad Reza Shah Pahlavi** online resource provides a biography of the Shah and this photo of Mohammad Reza Shah Pahlavi and his first wife, Arya Mehr.

They encouraged other countries to do the same. Since most of the skilled oil workers had been British, oil production in Iran came to a near standstill.

Mossadegh made the United States nervous. Americans feared he would overthrow the shah and form a pro-Soviet nation. The United States and the Soviet Union were enemies fighting the Cold War. They did not fight any actual battles, but they walked a tightrope. A misstep could end in nuclear war. Both the Americans and Soviets had nuclear weapons. These weapons gave them the power to destroy one another. With these fears in mind, President Dwight D. Eisenhower agreed to help

▲ This was the flag of Iran from the 1950s until the Islamic Revolution in 1979. Some form of this "lion and sun" flag was used in Persia for centuries.

the British. America's Central Intelligence Agency (CIA) launched an undercover coup. It was code-named Operation Ajax. The CIA worked with the shah to oust Mossadegh. They removed him from office in August 1953. Mossadegh lived the rest of his life under house arrest. The shah richly rewarded the United States. The United States now had a 40 percent stake in Iran's oil industry. Iranians lost their dreams of fully controlling Iran's oil profits. When Iranians learned of the United State's doings, they were angry. Iranians would distrust the United States for years to come.[2]

▶ The Shah's White Revolution

With American support, Shah Mohammad Reza Pahlavi proposed social and economic reforms. He hoped to bring about revolutionary change without revolutionary violence. He called his plan the White Revolution. Women and many non-Muslims gained the right to vote. More people learned to read and write. Landowners were forced to sell land to the state. The state then gave the land to farmers. Religious conservatives did not like some of these changes. Some religious leaders were landowners who lost money in the land reforms. Iran's holy city of Qom became the center for Shi'a opposition to the shah. Qom is an educational center for Shi'a Muslim study. One of Qom's religious scholars was Ayatollah Khomeini. Khomeini was an intense and charismatic man. When he spoke, people listened. He was outspoken in his disgust for the shah's leadership. In 1964, the shah forced Khomeini to leave the country.

The shah did not allow people to disagree with him. He outlawed any political parties if they opposed him. He restricted what journalists could print and broadcast. Most frightening was his secret police force, SAVAK. Using torture and violence, the secret police cracked down on anyone who dared to voice a different opinion.

▶ Revolution!

After he left the country, Ayatollah Khomeini had more freedom to speak his mind. He spent time in Iraq, and then settled in Paris. Meanwhile, the shah spent Iran's money on extravagant events. In 1971, he hosted an

▲ Supreme leader Ayatollah Khomeini greets the crowd before voting in Iran's 1988 parliamentary elections. Khomeini had been a popular figure in Iran since the 1960s.

expensive party for foreign dignitaries. The occasion was the 2,500th anniversary of the creation of the Persian Empire. The shah built a huge city of tents outside the ruins of Persepolis. He spent $3 million on this event, while Iranians in northern Iran suffered through a horrible famine.[3]

Oil prices hit an all-time high in 1974. Little of Iran's oil profits benefited ordinary citizens. The shah spent most of it building up his stockpile of weapons. In the late 1970s, oil prices plummeted. Iran's economy was crippled, leaving people without work. Huge crowds of Iranians took to the streets. The shah responded by ordering everyone to return home. He put the military on the streets and banned further demonstrations. The people did not obey. On September 8, 1978, the army fired into a large crowd gathered in Tehran. The crowd fought back and more than six hundred people were killed. The violent day was named Black Friday. Ayatollah Khomeini became more active as the leader of the opposition movement. He demanded that the shah leave Iran. The shah and his wife fled to Egypt in January 1979. A few days later, Ayatollah Khomeini returned to Iran. People of many different backgrounds had joined together to depose the shah. Now only one question remained: What would the new government look like?

▶ The American Embassy: Nest of Spies

In the aftermath of the revolution, Iranian university students shocked the world. The students stormed into the United States embassy in Tehran. They took Americans

The Islamic National Guard marches in support of Ayatollah Khomeini not long after he took power in 1979.

In 1953, the Central Intelligence Agency was involved in a covert operation to overthrow the Iranian government. This *New York Times* Web site provides extensive coverage on this operation.

Access this Web site from http://www.myreportlinks.com

hostage. They said they would release the staff on one condition: The United States had to hand over the shah. Shah Pahlavi was dying of cancer. He was receiving medical treatment in the United States. Iranians wanted the shah to face trial in Iran. Iranians also remembered the CIA coup from the 1950s. They feared the United States might meddle in Iran's affairs again.[4] The Iranians had worked together to overthrow Shah Mohammad Reza Pahlavi. Now they wanted to make their own decisions, without any Western interference. The students declared they had uncovered a "nest of spies." Ayatollah Khomeini treated the students like heroes, not criminals. No one dreamed the standoff would last as long as it did. A painstaking 444 days passed before the Americans

▲ An American hostage is bound at the wrists and blindfolded while being displayed to the crowd outside of the U.S. Embassy in Tehran. Sixty Americans were held hostage for 444 days.

were released. President Jimmy Carter refused to negotiate with the hostage takers. He planned a secret operation to rescue the Americans. The rescue was a humiliating failure. An American helicopter and plane crashed in the desert on the way to Tehran. Eight American military men died. The hostage crisis was a blow to President Carter's career. In the next election, President Carter lost to Ronald Reagan. Eventually the United States agreed to give back to Iran $8 billion in Iranian assets that the Americans had frozen in return for the hostages. The

Americans came home five days after President Reagan took the oath of office.

▶ The Islamic Republic of Iran

Ayatollah Khomeini had a strong voice during the revolution. With the shah gone, he became the supreme leader of the new Islamic Republic of Iran. His young government adopted a new constitution based on Islamic law. They restructured the government and created new positions. The parliament remained. Now there was an elected president, an appointed prime minister, and a Council of Guardians who would be selected by the supreme leader. The Council of Guardians had twelve members: six lawyers and six religious scholars. The Council had sweeping powers. They would decide who

Islamic Republic of Iran Broadcasting, or IRIB for short, is a leading news agency covering the country of Iran. Its easy-to-use site allows you to search for past news articles.

Access this Web site from http://www.myreportlinks.com

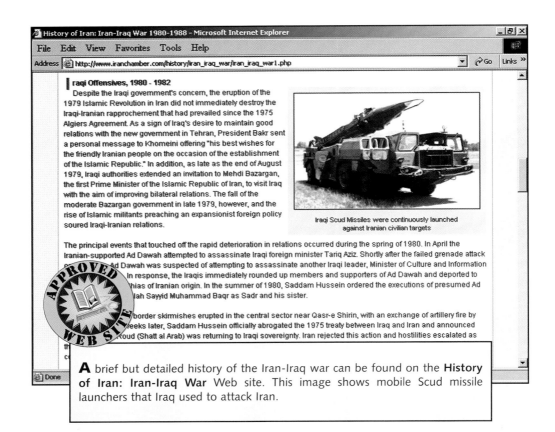

Iraqi Offensives, 1980 - 1982

Despite the Iraqi government's concern, the eruption of the 1979 Islamic Revolution in Iran did not immediately destroy the Iraqi-Iranian rapprochement that had prevailed since the 1975 Algiers Agreement. As a sign of Iraq's desire to maintain good relations with the new government in Tehran, President Bakr sent a personal message to Khomeini offering "his best wishes for the friendly Iranian people on the occasion of the establishment of the Islamic Republic." In addition, as late as the end of August 1979, Iraqi authorities extended an invitation to Mehdi Bazargan, the first Prime Minister of the Islamic Republic of Iran, to visit Iraq with the aim of improving bilateral relations. The fall of the moderate Bazargan government in late 1979, however, and the rise of Islamic militants preaching an expansionist foreign policy soured Iraqi-Iranian relations.

Iraqi Scud Missiles were continuously launched against Iranian civilian targets

The principal events that touched off the rapid deterioration in relations occurred during the spring of 1980. In April the Iranian-supported Ad Dawah attempted to assassinate Iraqi foreign minister Tariq Aziz. Shortly after the failed grenade attack [Ad] Dawah was suspected of attempting to assassinate another Iraqi leader, Minister of Culture and Information [...] In response, the Iraqis immediately rounded up members and supporters of Ad Dawah and deported to [...] hias of Iranian origin. In the summer of 1980, Saddam Hussein ordered the executions of presumed Ad [Dawa]h Sayyid Muhammad Baqr as Sadr and his sister.

[...] border skirmishes erupted in the central sector near Qasr-e Shirin, with an exchange of artillery fire by [...] eeks later, Saddam Hussein officially abrogated the 1975 treaty between Iraq and Iran and announced [...] oud (Shatt al Arab) was returning to Iraqi sovereignty. Iran rejected this action and hostilities escalated as

A brief but detailed history of the Iran-Iraq war can be found on the **History of Iran: Iran-Iraq War** Web site. This image shows mobile Scud missile launchers that Iraq used to attack Iran.

could run in elections. They could veto any laws they thought went against Islam.

It surprised many people when Ayatollah Khomeini established a government ruled by a very strict religious elite. This type of government is called a theocracy. Certainly not all the protesters had been Islamic conservatives. Many Iranians had imagined a new Iran where they would be free to speak their minds. New laws included strict dress codes for women. The laws forced many women to give up their careers and stay at home. Universities closed down. When they reopened, women were barred from some subjects. Women could no longer study in the same classrooms as men. People protested these restrictions. The government responded with violent crackdowns. Iran had not gained political freedom after all.

The Iran-Iraq War

Iraq invaded Iran in September 1980. Iraq's leader, Saddam Hussein, hoped for a quick victory. After all, Iran's government was very inexperienced and the army was in disarray. However, Iran is a much bigger country than Iraq. Iran rallied and put up a strong fight. By 1982, Iran had pushed the Iraqis back to the border. The war did not end there. Iran began penetrating Iraqi territory. Ayatollah Khomeini vowed to spread the Islamic Revolution to Iraq. At first the United States government was a neutral party. After 1982, the United States officially supported Iraq. The United States put pressure on other countries to stop selling weapons to Iran. In 1986, a secret leaked out. The United States government had quietly been selling weapons to Iran. This went against the United States' own policy. The resulting scandal was known as Irangate, or the Iran-Contra Scandal. In 1988, Iran and Iraq finally agreed to, and signed, a cease-fire sponsored by the United Nations. Over one million soldiers had died in the war.

Iranians Voters Struggle to be Heard

Ayatollah Khomeini died in 1989. He was ninety-one years old. The day of his death, June 4, is celebrated as a national holiday. Ten million mourners attended his

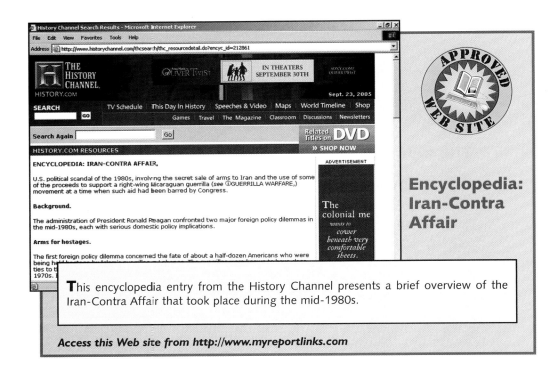

Encyclopedia: Iran-Contra Affair

This encyclopedia entry from the History Channel presents a brief overview of the Iran-Contra Affair that took place during the mid-1980s.

Access this Web site from http://www.myreportlinks.com

funeral. The hearse carrying his coffin was unable to move through the huge crowds. In the end a helicopter carried the body of the popular leader to his tomb. After his death, the Council of Experts elected Ayatollah Ali Khamenei as the new supreme leader. He had been the preferred choice of Khomeini.

With the founder of the republic gone, Iranian society began to loosen some of its strictest laws. In the 1997 presidential election, Iranians voted for change. They elected pro-reform candidate Mohammed Khatami. President Khatami renewed contact with Western countries. He gave the press more freedom of speech. He wanted to make the government less secretive. In 2000, Iranians continued to vote for politicians that supported change. They elected many pro-reform candidates to parliament. Most parliament members supported Khatami's ideas. The powerful Council of Guardians blocked their path. They threw out any laws they did not agree with. In the 2004 elections, the Council barred pro-reform candidates from running. Discouraged, many Iranians did not bother to vote.

Conservative Muslims gained a majority in the parliament. Khatami was powerless to enact his ideas because everyone knew he would not be president for much longer.[5] On June 25, 2005, Iranian voters elected a conservative named Mahmoud Ahmadinejad to be the new president.

Mahmoud Ahmadinejad surprisingly won the Iranian presidential election in June 2005. On this BBC Web site, you will find his biography. You can also view a video clip with more background information.

Access this Web site from http://www.myreportlinks.com

Land and Climate

Iran is a place of dramatic contrasts. The center of the country is an elevated, flat land with great expanses of deserts and salt marshes. A ring of rugged mountain ranges surrounds the interior deserts. Outside the ring of mountains are two flat, coastal plains. One plain borders the Caspian Sea to the north. The other plain runs along the Persian Gulf in the south.

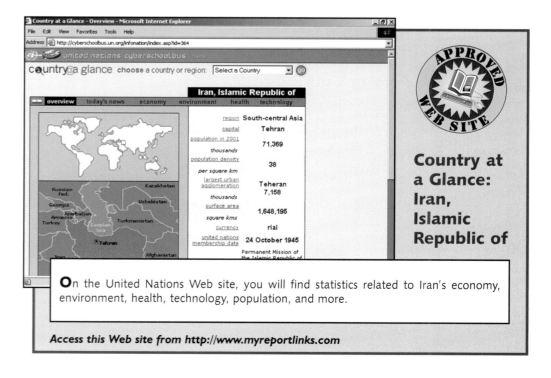

Country at a Glance: Iran, Islamic Republic of

On the United Nations Web site, you will find statistics related to Iran's economy, environment, health, technology, population, and more.

Access this Web site from http://www.myreportlinks.com

Iran has three major climate zones: arid, semiarid, and subtropical. Nearly half of Iran has an arid desert climate. It receives less than 4 inches of precipitation each year. Precipitation is water that falls to the earth in the form of rain, mist, hail, sleet, or snow. Most of the country is semiarid. Semiarid climates receive more water than the arid deserts. Still, not all of this precipitation is useful. Some is in the form of snow high in the mountains where few people live. Seasons in the semiarid regions can be extreme. The Persian Gulf in particular is known for its difficult climate. In the summer, temperatures can reach 120°F. Winters are more comfortable, with an average temperature of 78°F.[1] Only the Caspian Sea region receives enough rainfall to be considered a subtropical climate. More than 40 inches of rain falls there each year. The Caspian Sea is the world's largest inland body of water.

The Persian Gulf

To Iran's south lies the great Persian Gulf, which is a shallow part of the Indian Ocean. It separates Iran from the Arabian peninsula to the south. The title Persian Gulf is often used to describe not only the Persian Gulf itself, but also its outlets: the Strait of Hormuz and the Gulf of Oman. The Gulf of Oman opens into the Arabian Sea, which drains into the Indian Ocean. Throughout history, the Persian Gulf has been an important route for people transporting goods from the Middle East to other parts of the world. Traders of the past had a difficult task when it came to moving goods overland. Iran is not easy to travel across. There are very few rivers that do not dry up in the summer months. Only one river, the Karun, may be navigated by boat, and then only for a short distance. Crossing the large, central deserts was nearly impossible until recent times. The sandy terrain, a lack of freshwater, and dangerous salt marshes made for tough travel

▲ *The Persian Gulf is an important body of water. Many goods are transported across the Gulf, and the seabed is rich in oil.*

conditions. The towering mountain ranges are another obstacle. More than two thirds of Iran's land is remote and unlivable. The conditions are just too rough for people to live there.[2]

One of the Most Mountainous Countries in the World

Iran is home to two major mountain ranges: the Elburz and the Zagros. Other mountains rise along the eastern border of Iran, near Afghanistan and Pakistan. Still more mountains rise in the northwest, along the border with Azerbaijan. Iran's mountains formed when parts of the earth's crust collided. Geologists—scientists who study the earth—know that our planet's outer crust is made up of about a dozen large pieces, called tectonic plates. These plates are slowly moving. Sometimes they bump

Postcards from Iran

This Web site provides a brief look at contemporary life in Iran. Learn about parties, traffic, cybercafes, and more.

Access this Web site from http://www.myreportlinks.com

into or rub against one another. When that happens, rock can be forced upward to the surface of the earth. This rock forms mountains. Iran has so many mountains because it sits directly above where three major pieces of crust meet.

Elburz and Zagros Mountain Ranges

The Elburz Range is located to the south of the Caspian Sea. Cliffs, visible from the seashore, rise straight up in the air for thousands of feet. It is a sight to behold. The wall of mountains forms a barrier that prevents clouds from moving through. Rain clouds from the Caspian Sea dump their water on the mountainsides. This creates the lush, subtropical climate in the land between the mountains and the Caspian Sea. The Elburz Mountains separate the Caspian region from Iran's large central plateau. A plateau is land that is shaped like a table—flat on top and raised up higher than the surrounding area. For that reason plateaus are sometimes called tablelands. The capital city, Tehran, sits on the plateau to the south of the mountains. Iran's tallest peak, Mount Damavand, stands guard over Tehran. This dormant volcano towers above all at 18,714 feet. These southern Elburz Mountains are much drier than those facing the Caspian Sea. At one time, these mountainsides were covered with forests of juniper trees. The junipers can withstand the cold temperatures and little rainfall of the region. They are very hearty, but grow very slowly under these poor conditions. When juniper forests are cut, they take a long time to grow back. People have overharvested the juniper

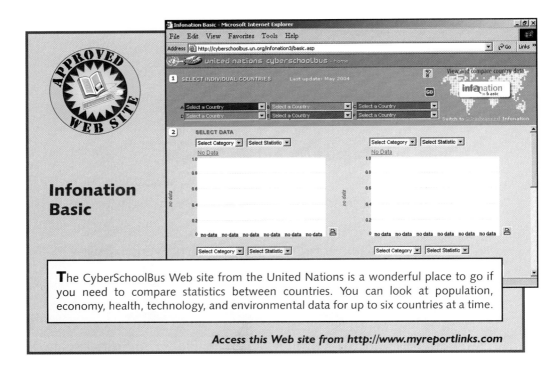

The CyberSchoolBus Web site from the United Nations is a wonderful place to go if you need to compare statistics between countries. You can look at population, economy, health, technology, and environmental data for up to six countries at a time.

Access this Web site from http://www.myreportlinks.com

trees for fuel. Today the juniper forests only survive in the highest elevations.[3]

The Zagros Range is a long and wide chain of mountains. They run in a diagonal line from Lake Urmia in the northwest down to the Gulf of Oman in the southwest. The Zagros cover a total distance in length of about six hundred miles. Here again the mountains' high altitudes block the path of rain clouds. Lush, jungle-like forests thrive in all the rainfall caught on the western slopes. Drier grasslands cover most of the eastern slopes. Persian language and culture began in the Fars region of the southwest Zagros. The ruins of the ancient city Persepolis stand here. The city of Shiraz is 40 miles from Persepolis. The poet Hafez wrote his beloved poems in Shiraz.

▶ Tremors and Quakes

Earthquakes are very common in Iran for the same reason Iran has many mountains. Earthquakes occur when pieces of the earth's crust shift, bump, or move. Iran sits on a hotbed of plate activity. The disturbance takes place far underground, but the effects of an earthquake are often felt on the surface. More than twenty major earthquakes hit Iran in the last hundred years. The most recent large-scale disaster occurred in 2003 when a major earthquake demolished the ancient city of Bam. The earthquake destroyed 70 percent of Bam's buildings. Nearly thirty thousand people were killed. Sadly, there is little education about earthquakes and the prevention of

▲ Snow has fallen on these desert sand dunes in Northern Iran. The temperature can fluctuate drastically in the Iranian deserts.

earthquake disasters. While there are building codes, they are not very strict and are rarely enforced.[4] "Most people think that what God wills will happen. This is absolutely wrong. This thinking is poisonous," said Tehran University professor Bahram Akasheh.[5]

Deserts of the Central Plateau

The Iranian plateau sits in the center of Iran, surrounded by mountains. The land is very dry and hot. Two huge deserts, the Dasht-e Kavir and Dasht-e Lut, cover most of the region. These deserts are all that remain of two ancient saltwater lakes. Dasht-e Lut is 300 miles long and 200 miles wide. It forms the eastern border of the central plateau. Its name means the Desert of Emptiness. Dasht-e Kavir, or the Great Salt Desert, is located in the northern part of the plateau. It is 500 miles long and 200 miles wide. At its center is the Kavir Buzurg, or the Great Kavir. The word kavir means salt marsh. Gooey brine lies beneath large crusty plates of salt. Brine is water that contains a lot of salt. The salt draws moisture from the air and ground. The salt desert behaves like quicksand, making it extremely dangerous to approach. Much of it remains unexplored. For hundreds of years there has been just one road through these deserts, but times are changing. People are forging new paths through this unexplored territory with heavy trucks. There is one animal that thrives in Iran's desert climate: the Asiatic cheetah. In the past, the cheetahs lived throughout West Asia, as far east as India. Today they are endangered. Asiatic cheetahs remain only in Iran's Dasht-e Kavir.

▲ *A shepherdess tends to her flock on the plains of Iran.*

The cheetah's fate is uncertain. The government has set aside protected reserves for the animals. However they also sell hunting permits to shoot cheetahs.

▶ Iranian Plains

Iran has two areas of coastal plains. Plains are large, unbroken areas of flat land. They are often used for agriculture and farming. The Khuzistan plain runs along southwestern Iran. At its southern end it borders the Persian Gulf. This plain is really part of the fertile Mesopotamian plains to the west in Iraq. The area from the Mediterranean Sea to the Persian Gulf is known as the Fertile Crescent. People have grown food crops here for thousands of years. Along the Persian Gulf, date palms, banana trees, and mangrove trees thrive in the scorching hot climate. Winds from the Persian Gulf bring moisture to the air, making it quite humid. Iran's other coastal plain is a narrow strip of land in the north by the Caspian Sea. The 400-mile-long plain sits between the Caspian Sea and the Elburz Mountains. At its narrowest, it is just 10 miles wide. In places the plain stretches to 70 miles wide. Unlike the rest of the country, it rains there constantly.

▲ *Each year thousands of flamingos nest at Lake Urmia in northwestern Iran.*

▶ Bodies of Water

For a country of deserts, Iran is blessed with water. To the north of the country is the huge Caspian Sea. Five major rivers empty into the Caspian, but none flows out from it. The water is salty, though less salty than the world's oceans. Four other countries also border the Caspian Sea: Azerbaijan, Turkmenistan, Russia, and Kazakhstan. All four of these countries belonged to the former Soviet Union. The Caspian Sea is about to become more developed. Scientists have discovered oil under the sea. It will not be long before oil companies are drilling into the seafloor. Drilling and development will inevitably cause pollution. Pollution will take a toll on the animals and fish that live in the Caspian.

Lake Urmia is a large salt lake located high in the remote northwest mountains. It is too salty for fish to live in, but algae and brine shrimp thrive there. Lake Urmia is an important breeding ground for many birds, including greater flamingos that feed on the shrimp. As many as twenty-five thousand pairs of flamingos meet at the lake to mate each spring. The climate here is extreme. It is hot and dry in the summer and bitterly cold in winter. The people of this region are nomadic animal herders. *Nomadic* means they move around, instead of settling in one place. The herders must find grass for their animals to eat. In the summer the herds graze in the grassy highlands. They move down to the low, protected valleys in the winter. Today's nomads are following in the footsteps of their ancestors. Domesticated sheep trace their ancestry to wild sheep from this region.

Economy and Agriculture

Today the Persian Gulf is best known for one thing: oil. The British first discovered reservoirs of oil there in 1908. Crude oil, or petroleum, is a chemical substance that comes from underground. It takes millions of years to make petroleum. It begins with sea organisms that settle into the sand on the ocean floor when they die. Over time they decompose and form crude oil. To remove the petroleum from underground, companies drill a well. A large, mechanical pump extracts the crude oil from the well. Then the oil goes to a plant called an oil refinery. The oil must be processed and refined before people can use it. The Persian Gulf is not only a source of oil, but it is also a route to carry oil to the rest of the world. Huge ships called oil tankers transport the oil out of the Middle East. They take the oil to ports around the world.

▶ A Wealth of Oil

Oil is in high demand in industrial countries. These countries have many factories, businesses, and vehicles that use oil. When oil burns, it releases energy. Machines need energy to fuel them. We use oil for many things. We heat buildings with furnaces that burn oil. Your family car runs on gasoline. Gas is a form of refined oil. Other

▲ Drilling for oil is an extremely important industry in Iran, and throughout much of the Middle East. This drilling rig is lit up at night.

vehicles, like planes, trains, buses, and tractors, all run on refined oil. Petroleum is also an ingredient in many modern things. Petroleum is an ingredient in plastics, paints, pharmaceuticals, crop fertilizers, and building materials. Oil is very valuable because so many people depend on it. Sometimes people call it "black gold."

Vast oil reserves sit under both the Persian Gulf and the Caspian Sea. Today, Iran is one of several nations that owns the Persian Gulf oil. Iraq, Kuwait, Saudi Arabia, and the United Arab Emirates are other oil-rich nations. The Persian Gulf has 60 percent of the world's oil reserves.[1] Iran alone has reserves of 125 billion barrels of oil. This is equal to 10 percent of the world's total reserves. Iran pumps nearly 4 million barrels of oil each day. Before the revolution, Iran removed 6 million

This BBC site contains a brief overview of Iran's neighbor country Iraq. Included are time lines of Iraq's history and key events for Iraqi Kurds. Iraq is one of many nations that also owns the Persian Gulf's oil.

Access this Web site from http://www.myreportlinks.com

barrels a day. The Iran-Iraq war of the 1980s hurt Iran's oil industry. Iraq bombed many oil sites in southern Iran. Iran is reconstructing, but oil production has not recovered to prerevolution levels. Iran also has huge reserves of natural gas. Natural gas is another source of energy. Americans use natural gas to cook food and heat homes. Iran has not tapped into the full potential of its natural gas wealth. To do so the country would need to spend a lot of money to develop its natural gas industry.

Oil is a nonrenewable resource. One day we will have used up all the earth's oil. This day is not so far away. Some predict it will be gone within a decade or two. Once it is gone, we will need an alternative energy source. So far scientists have not discovered a man-made, petroleum-like fuel. As the earth's remaining oil reserves dwindle, countries that own oil will have an advantage. They will be able to get high prices for any oil they are willing to sell.

The Price of Luxury

The Caspian Sea is known for another kind of "black gold:" caviar. Caviar is a salty, richly flavored gourmet food. Fish eggs may sound unappealing to you, but food lovers are willing to pay top price for good caviar. Iran controls 50 percent of the Caspian Sea caviar market. The eggs of a Caspian beluga sturgeon can fetch up to $160 per ounce. The beluga sturgeon is an ancient species. Scientists believe it was already swimming in lakes when the dinosaurs roamed the earth. But the sturgeon, which can live to be one hundred years old, may

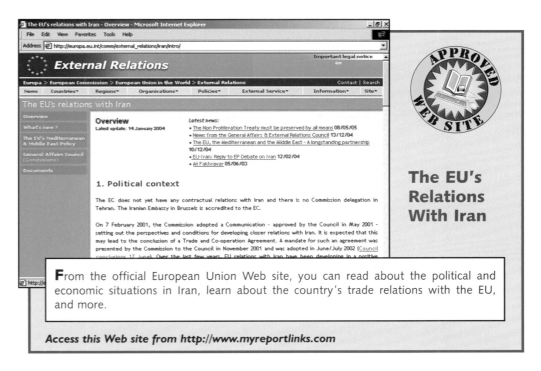

From the official European Union Web site, you can read about the political and economic situations in Iran, learn about the country's trade relations with the EU, and more.

Access this Web site from http://www.myreportlinks.com

be in danger. New research shows beluga sturgeon numbers are falling fast. Poaching, or catching the fish illegally, is a major concern. The United States imports a lot of caviar from the Caspian Sea region. In 2005, the United States made a demand of Iran and all other countries that export caviar to the United States. They must show the United States what they are doing to help the beluga sturgeon. Environmentalists say this is not enough. They argue that only a full ban on caviar could make a difference.[2]

Iran has exported its celebrated rugs for centuries. The Safavid leader Shah Abbas made rug weaving into a royal craft. He invested in rug factories in his capital city of Esfahan and encouraged trade with other countries. Today, rug making remains a popular handcraft in Iran.

For a short while after the 1979 revolution, the religious leaders could not export rugs to Western countries because of United States sanctions against them. Times have since changed. U.S. President Bill Clinton lifted the ban on importing the rugs. Iran once again sells Persian rugs for the entire world to enjoy. The industry brings in millions of dollars to Iran's economy each year.

▲ A farmer is bringing crops to market near the border of Iran and Afghanistan.

▶ A Drug Problem

Iran's eastern deserts and mountains are a wild frontier. Few people live in Sistan and Baluchistan. These two provinces border Afghanistan and Pakistan. Illegal drug smugglers take advantage of the lack of a police presence in the area along Iran's eastern border. These outlaws slip across the border from Afghanistan, where drug lords grow fields of opium poppies. Opium poppies are the source of illicit drugs called opiates. Heroin, a highly addictive drug, is an opiate. Smugglers transport the drugs to Europe and sell them illegally on the black market. Iran is trying to address the problem, but it needs help. It is up against wealthy drug lords armed with high-tech weapons. Stopping the flow of drugs from Afghanistan into Iran should be a priority for the world community. As much as 90 percent of Europe's heroin comes from Afghanistan.[3]

▶ Too Many People, Too Few Jobs

After the revolution, the government encouraged people to have large families. During the 1980s, the average family had six children. The 30 million babies born that decade doubled the country's population.[4] Today 70 percent of the population is under the age of thirty. The average age is only twenty-three. Iran's economy did not grow as fast as its population. As a result, many young adults cannot find work. In 2003, Iran reported that 16 percent of its population was unemployed. Many experts speculate that the number is probably higher, close to 20 percent. There are just not enough jobs to go around.

Another problem is underemployment. This means that a person can only find a job that is beneath his or her skill and education level. For example, a doctor would be underemployed if she can only find work as a house-keeper. Many young adults cannot afford to rent or own a house. They share a home with their parents well into adulthood. They may save money for many years before they can afford their own home.

▲ *Newly elected Iranian president Mahmoud Ahmadinejad (center). On the left is Hassan Khomeini, grandson of Grand Ayatollah Ruhollah Khomeini. One of the challenges President Ahmadinejad will face is the problem of high unemployment.*

▶Irrigation: Bringing Water to the Fields

Iran is a semiarid country. Fifteen percent of the land at most can be used for agriculture. To grow food crops on the dry central plateau, farmers need additional water. The Persians figured out a good way to solve this problem long ago. They built irrigation systems called qanats. The qanats are underground channels. They bring water from the hills to the fields. Built on a slope, they use only gravity to move the water. Key crops include wheat, sugar beets, sugarcane, potatoes, rice, corn, soybeans, and bananas. Iran exports pistachios, flowers, and dates to other countries. Traditionally, wealthy landlords owned the agricultural land. Peasant farmers rented the land. Farming involved backbreaking labor. With the landlord making the profits, farmers had no way to get ahead. When the farmers began to abandon the countryside for city life, the government stepped in. During the shah's White Revolution of the 1960s, some farmers gained better rights. After the revolution, agriculture underwent even more reform. Yet with the population explosion, Iran is unable to produce enough food to feed everyone. The population depends on imported food from other countries.

▶Government Handouts

In today's economy, many Iranians cannot afford to buy food and gas. Forty percent of Iranians live below the poverty level. To address this problem, the government provides subsidies. This means the government gives

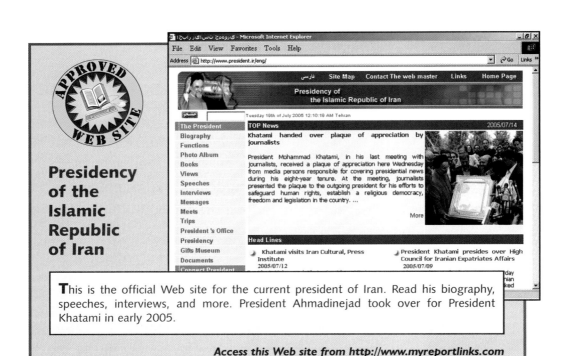

Presidency of the Islamic Republic of Iran

This is the official Web site for the current president of Iran. Read his biography, speeches, interviews, and more. President Ahmadinejad took over for President Khatami in early 2005.

Access this Web site from http://www.myreportlinks.com

people groceries and gas at low cost. For instance, in 2004, Americans paid over two dollars per gallon of gas at the pump. That same year, Iranians were outraged when the Majles voted to increase gas prices to a mere ninety-five cents (U.S. dollars) per gallon. The subsidies do help citizens in the short term. In the long run, they hurt the government by draining its bank accounts. Iran could better spend the money it wastes on subsidies. It could use the money to improve the economy. Then more Iranians could find jobs. With good jobs, Iranians could afford to pay full price for food and gasoline. This would be a difficult change to make. Getting rid of the subsidies would not be popular with the people they now help.

▶ Looking Toward the Future: Economic Reform

Iran's economy depends very heavily on the oil industry. Oil profits make up over 50 percent of all government revenue. In 2005, oil prices were high. Iran's oil brings the country great wealth. Yet it is not healthy for an economy to depend so much on any one industry. To have a stronger economy, Iran should develop other industries as well. Iranian leaders such as former President Khatami have been trying to make changes to Iran's economy. The religious conservatives are against it, as well as Khatami's other reform ideas. It would take money to build up other industries. Iran would need the help of foreign investors. The ruling conservatives do not want foreigners involved in their economy. They may not have much choice. In 2002, the country passed legislation encouraging foreign investment.

Iran is locked out from the world's most powerful economy. The United States, citing Iran's support of international terrorism, refuses to do business with Iran. President Bill Clinton first established an embargo against Iran in 1995. In 2000, Iranians voted in a new Majles with many people who supported reform. The United States responded by lifting bans on the import of carpets, nuts, and caviar from Iran. After the conservatives retook the Majles, President George W. Bush extended the embargo into the foreseeable future.

It is possible Iran may not need the United States. It may just have to look for another market with money to spend. China has the world's fastest growing economy. Iran and China recently signed a huge oil and natural

▲ *An Iran Air jet about to take off. The leadership of Iran is looking to promote tourism and strengthen other areas of the country's economy to provide its people with a brighter future.*

gas business deal. It is a good match. Iran needs the money to invest in its economy. China is sorely lacking in energy sources. The United States embargo may lose its potency with China in the picture.[5] Iraq is a wild card in the deck. The Bush administration hopes to build a successful democracy in Iraq. If that happens, the people of Iran may be inspired to overthrow their religious leaders. The United States would welcome a new government in Iran. It would almost certainly be more friendly to the United States than the Islamic Republic.

Report Links

The Internet sites described below can be accessed at http://www.myreportlinks.com

▶**Country Profile: Iran**
Editor's Choice The BBC provides an overview of this Middle Eastern country.

▶**Islamic Republic News Agency**
Editor's Choice Read the daily news from Iran and the rest of the Middle East.

▶**Perry-Castañeda Library Map Collection: Iran Maps**
Editor's Choice View historical and present-day maps of Iran at this Web site.

▶**Background Note: Iran**
Editor's Choice The U.S. Department of State Web site has an informative section about Iran.

▶**Iran: Political Struggle**
Editor's Choice Get a closer look into the current state of Iran.

▶***The World Factbook:* Iran**
Editor's Choice Information from the CIA's Web site on Iran.

▶**Ayatollah Khomeini**
An online biography of the former leader of Iran, Ayatollah Khomeini.

▶**BBC News: Middle East**
Read the latest news from the Middle East.

▶**CNN: World/Middle East**
CNN.com has the latest news from Iran and the Middle East.

▶**County at a Glance: Iran, Islamic Republic of**
Glean information on Iran from the United Nations Web site.

▶**Country Profile: Iraq**
Learn about Iran's neighboring country.

▶**A Country Study: Iran**
The Library of Congress Web site contains an overview of Iran.

▶**Encyclopedia: Iran-Contra Affair**
Read about the Iran-Contra scandal, part of which involved the secret sale of arms to Iran.

▶**The EU's Relations With Iran**
Learn about Iran's relationship with the European Union.

▶**History of Iran: Iran-Iraq War 1980–1988**
A Web resource about the war between Iran and Iraq.

Report Links

The Internet sites described below can be accessed at http://www.myreportlinks.com

▶**Infonation Basic**
The United Nations provides data about the countries of the world.

▶**Iran: Forbidden Iran, January 2004**
A journalist risks her life to expose the seldom seen side of Iran.

▶*Iran Daily*
Read national and international news articles from this daily Iranian news site.

▶**Iranian Culture & Religions**
Articles dealing with cultural and religious events and issues can be found here.

▶**IRIB News**
The Islamic Republic of Iran Broadcasting Web site.

▶**Mohammad Reza Shah Pahlavi**
Read an online biography of the last king of Iran.

▶**Postcards from Iran**
Get a look into contemporary life in Iran from this Web site.

▶**Presidency of the Islamic Republic of Iran**
Find out about the current president of Iran.

▶**Profile: Mahmoud Ahmadinejad**
A brief biography of the recently elected president of Iran.

▶**Salam Iran**
On this Web site you will find valuable information on Iran.

▶**Secrets of History: The C.I.A. in Iran**
Learn about the plot to overthrow the Iranian government and the CIA's role in that plan.

▶*Tehran Times*
Read the daily paper from Iran's capital city.

▶*TIME* **Trail: Iran**
A look into the recent history of Iran from *Time* magazine.

▶**Timeline of Art History: Iran**
Click on the time line to see artifacts from the Iranian region from 8000 B.C. to the present.

▶*Vis à Vis: Beyond the Veil*
Find out about Iranian culture on this PBS site.

Allah—The Arabic word for God.

Armenians—A group of people originally from the area that is now divided between the countries of Iran, Armenia, and Turkey.

Aryans—People descended from those who speak Indo-European languages.

ayatollah—A rank in the Shi'a religious leadership.

Azeri—A group of people that originated in what is now the country called Azerbaijan.

Baha'i—A religion that began in Iran during the 1800s.

Baluchis—A group of people that originated in the area that is now Southeast Iran and Northwest Pakistan.

chador—A traditional Persian garment that covers a woman from head to toe.

conservative—A person who values tradition and opposes change.

coup—A sudden overthrow of a government.

daeva—Ancient gods and goddesses of Iran.

diplomacy—Negotiations or relations between two nations.

Farsi—*See* Persian.

hajj—Pilgrimage to Mecca.

hejab—Iran's legal dress code for women.

hostage—A person who is held captive.

Islam—A major world religion based on the Qur'an.

Kurds—A group of people known for their agriculture that lives in a region that includes parts of Iran, Iraq, Turkey, Syria, Armenia, and Azerbaijan.

Majles—Iran's parliament.

Mecca—A city in Saudi Arabia, holy for Muslims.

Muslim—A person who follows Islam.

Persia—An old name for Iran.

Persian—The language of Iran. Also known as Farsi or Iranian.

Qur'an—The Islamic holy book: the word of Allah.

revolution—A changing of the leaders of a government as well as all the laws and rules in a society.

sanctions—Measures taken by a group of nations to punish another nation economically or through military force.

shah—The Persian word for king.

Shi'a—A branch of Islam with a large following in Iran.

Sunni—A branch of Islam.

Zoroastrianism—An ancient religion founded in Iran.

Chapter 1. Iran in the News

1. Judith Miller, *God Has Ninety-Nine Names* (New York: Simon and Schuster, 1996), p. 441.

2. President George W. Bush, "State of the Union Address 2002," *The White House,* n.d., <http://www.whitehouse.gov/news/releases/2002/01/print/20020129-11.html> (March 27, 2005).

3. BBC News, "Iran Tops US 'Trouble Spots' List," *BBC World News,* n.d., <http://news.bbb.co.uk/1/hi/world/middle_east/4193909.stm> (February 7, 2005).

4. James Fallows, "Will Iran Be Next?" *The Atlantic Monthly,* December 2004, p. 99.

Chapter 2. Introducing Iran

1. Merriam-Webster Online Dictionary, "paradise," *Etymology,* n.d., <http://www.m-w.com/cgi-bin/dictionary?book=Dictionary&va=paradise&x=7&y=13> (February 25, 2005).

2. Pejman Akbarzadeh, "Persia, the Thousand-Year-Old Name of Iran," *Iran Chamber Society,* n.d., <http://www.iranchamber.com/podium/history/031020_persia_thousandyearold_name.php> (March 12, 2005).

3. Nazila Fathi, "Israel 'must be wiped off the map,' Iran's Leader Says," *San Francisco Chronicle,* October 27, 2005, <http://www.sfgate.com/cgi-bin/article.cgi?file=/c/a/2005/10/27/MNGQFFEHG01.DTL> (November 1, 2005).

4. Kamin Mohammadi, "The Culture," *The Lonely Planet Guide to Iran* (Oakland, Calif.: Lonely Planet Publications, 2004), p. 50.

Chapter 3. Religion in Iran

1. Nima Sadjadi, "Zoroastrianism," *Farvardyn: An Illustrated Reference Portal about Ancient Persia,* n.d., <http://www.farvardyn.com/zoroaster.php> (March 20, 2005).

2. Elton L. Daniel, *The History of Iran* (Westport, Conn.: Greenwood Press, 2001), p. 30.

3. Terry C. Muck, "An Introduction to Islam: One God, Many Believers," *The Muslim World,* Geoffrey Orens, ed. (New York: H. W. Wilson, 2003), p. 5.

4. Daniel, p. 1.

5. Robert Stockman, "A History of Islam from a Baha'i Perspective," *Baha'i Library Online,* n.d., <http://Baha'i-library.com/unpubl.articles/islam.Baha'i.html> (December 12, 2004).

6. Reshma Memon Yaqub, "Hajj: The Journey of a Lifetime," *The Muslim World,* Geoffrey Orens, ed. (New York: H. W. Wilson, 2003), p. 27.

Chapter 4. Iranian Art and Culture

1. Kamin Mohammadi, "The Culture," *The Lonely Planet Guide to Iran* (Oakland, Calif.: Lonely Planet Publications, 2004), p. 41.

2. Massoume Price, "Festival of Fire, or Chahar Shanbeh Soori," *Iran Chamber Society*, n.d., <http://www.iranchamber.com/culture/articles/festival_of_fire.php> (March 11, 2005).

3. Iran Chamber Society, "No-Rooz, the Iranian New Year at Present Time," *Iran Chamber Society,* n.d., <http://www.iranchamber.com/culture/articles/norooz_iranian_new_year.php> (March 11, 2005).

4. Afshin Molavi, "A New Day in Iran?" *Smithsonian,* March 2005, p. 57.

5. Behzad Yaghmaian, "Iranian Distrust of America is 50 Years in the Making," *USA Today,* February 22, 2005, p. 13A.

6. BBC News, "Postcards from Iran: Surfing the Net," *BBC World News,* February 13, 2004, <http://news .bbc.co.uk/1/hi/world/middle_east/3486923.stm> (July 26, 2005).

7. Human Rights Watch, "Iran: Blogger Sentenced to 14 Years in Prison," *Human Rights Watch,* February 24, 2005, <http://hrw.org/english/docs/2005/02/23/ iran10204.htm> (March 26, 2005).

8. Economist, "Still Failing, Still Defiant," *Economist,* December 11, 2004, pp. 23–25.

Chapter 5. Early History

1. Elton L. Daniel, *The History of Iran* (Westport, Conn.: Greenwood Press, 2001), pp. 21–24.

2. Cyrus Shahmiri, "The Elamite Empire: 2700–644 bce," *Iran Chamber Society,* n.d., <http://www .iranchamber.com/history/elamite/elamite.php> (February 19, 2005).

3. Editors of Time-Life Books, *Persians: Masters of Empire* (Alexandria, Va.: Time-Life Books, 1995), pp. 59–60.

4. Daniel, p. 74.

5. Iran Chamber Society, "The History of Iran: Turks and Mongols," *Iran Chamber Society*, n.d., <http:// www.iranchamber.com/history/turks_mongols/turks _mongols.php> (March 4, 2005).

Chapter 6. Modern History

1. Iran Chamber Society, "History of Iran: Pahlavi Dynasty," *Iran Chamber Society,* n.d., <http://www.iranchamber.com/history/pahlavi/pahlavi.php> (March 15, 2005).

2. Behzad Yaghmaian, "Iranian Distrust of America is 50 Years in the Making," *USA Today,* February 22, 2005, p. 13A.

3. Judith Miller, *God Has Ninety-Nine Names* (New York: Simon and Schuster, 1996), p. 431.

4. Afshin Molavi, "A New Day in Iran?" *Smithsonian,* March 2005, p. 61.

5. Jim Muir, "Analysis: What Now For Iran?" *BBC World News,* February 23, 2004, <http://news.bbc.co.uk/1/hi/world/middle_east/3514551.stm> (July 26, 2005).

Chapter 7. Land and Climate

1. Andrew Burke, *Lonely Planet Guide: Iran* (Oakland, Calif.: Lonely Planet Publications, 2004), p. 260.

2. Elton L. Daniel, *The History of Iran* (Westport, Conn.: Greenwood Press, 2001), p. 5.

3. Julie Bourns, "Terrestrial Ecoregions: Elburz Range Forest Steppe," *World Wildlife Fund,* n.d., <http://www.worldwildlife.org/wildworld/profiles/terrestrial/pa/pa0507_full.html> (January 21, 2005).

4. Burke, p. 69.

5. BBC News, "Iran Earthquake Kills Thousands," *BBC World News,* n.d., <http://news.bbc.co.uk/2/hi/middle_east/3348613.stm> (January 21, 2005).

Chapter 8. Economy and Agriculture

1. The Canadian Embassy of the Islamic Republic of Iran, "Iran Info," *Salam Iran,* n.d.,<http://www.salamiran.org/IranInfo/General/Geography/> (February 14, 2005).

2. Christopher Pala, "New Trade Rules on Sturgeon," *Science,* March 11, 2005, vol. 307, p. 1545.

3. Andrew North, "Iran's Drugs War," *Middle East,* November 2000, pp. 8–9.

4. Andrew Burke, *Lonely Planet Guide: Iran* (Oakland, Calif.: Lonely Planet Publications, 2004), p. 36.

5. Vivienne West, "Iran Looks East," *Fortune,* February 21, 2005, p. 88.

Batmanglij, Najmieh. *New Food of Life: Ancient Persian and Modern Iranian Cooking and Ceremonies.* Washington, D.C.: Mage Publishers, 1992.

Doak. Robin S. *Iran.* Mankato, Minn.: Compass Point Books, 2004.

Greenblatt, Miriam. *Enchantment of the World: Iran.* New York: Children's Press, 2002.

Kheirabadi, Masoud. *Modern World Nations: Iran.* Broomall, Penn.: Chelsea House Publishers, 2003.

Nadler, Daniel. *Iran the Beautiful.* Washington, D.C.: Mage Publishers, 2002.

Nardo, Don. *Life During the Great Civilizations: Ancient Persia.* San Diego: Blackbirch Press, 2003.

Porter, Yves. *Palaces and Gardens of Persia.* Paris: Flammarion, 2004.

Thompson, Jan. *World Religions: Islam.* Vancouver: Whitecap Books, Ltd., 2005.

Tubb, Jonathan N. *Eyewitness Books: Bible Lands.* New York: DK Publishing, 2000.

Wilkinson, Philip. *Eyewitness Books: Islam.* New York: DK Publishing, 2002.

Willett, Edward. *Middle East Leaders: Ayatollah Khomeini.* New York: Rosen Publishing Group, 2004.